FAMILY-STYLE MEALS AT THE
Hali'imaile General Store

FAMILY-STYLE MEALS AT THE
Hali'imaile General Store

BEVERLY GANNON

with Joan Namkoong

Photography by Laurie Smith

TEN SPEED PRESS
Berkeley | Toronto

Ten Speed Press
PO Box 7123
Berkeley CA 94707
www.tenspeed.com

Distributed in Australia by Simon and Schuster Australia, in Canada by Ten Speed Press Canada, in New Zealand by Southern Publishers Group, in South Africa by Real Books, and in the United Kingdom and Europe by Publishers Group UK.

Jacket and text design by Toni Tajima
Food styling by Wesley Martin

Library of Congress Cataloging-in-Publication Data
Gannon, Beverly, 1949-
    Family-style meals at the Hali'imaile General Store /
Beverly Gannon with Joan Namkoong.
        p. cm.
    Includes index.
    ISBN-13: 978-1-58008-951-7
    ISBN-10: 1-58008-951-8
    1. Hawaiian cookery. 2. Hali'imaile General Store (Restaurant)
I. Namkoong, Joan. II. Title.
    TX724.5.H3G354 2009
    641.59969—dc22
                                    2008030196
Printed in China
First printing, 2009

1 2 3 4 5 6 7 8 9 10 — 13 12 11 10 09

Contents

Acknowledgments

WHEN I FINISHED MY FIRST BOOK almost eight years ago, I swore I would never write another one. I had not written anything since college essays. All the recipes were handwritten on yellow legal pads. I knew nothing about computers. It was the hardest thing I had ever done, including opening two restaurants and a catering business. It was more stressful than planning a party for five hundred or a lunch for the vice president of the United States.

But thousands of sold copies later, the stressful memories subsided, I learned the art of the computer, and I learned that people loved my first book. After years of watching family meals disappear, I thought how great it would be to have a book that encouraged families to cook and eat together once again. So here it is—another book. I can't believe it.

To my coauthor Joan Namkoong, thank you, thank you, thank you. You pushed me in the best possible way to get this book done! You can delete the "recipes???" message to me as of now. It was a pleasure to have you write this book with me. You are truly the ultimate "foodie" and a great friend.

To Michelle Kaina for all your hard work creating the dessert recipes for the home cook, a heartfelt *mahalo*. You are on the "Top 10" list of Best Employees Ever!

To food stylist Wes Martin, I love you. Who would have thought we would be doing two books together? You are the only person I can imagine letting destroy my brand-new kitchen to test all the recipes. I'll remember you every time I look in the oven. Your food styling is incredible. You deserve to have all you wish for because you give that away to everyone you work with. I can't wait for more eat-a-thons in NYC. *Mahalo nui loa.*

To photographer Laurie Smith—two books together! You are the best. Your photos of the families of Maui—not to mention your fabulous food shots—capture exactly what I wanted for the book. It is all about family life and you made it happen. Many *mahalos*.

Thanks to my publisher Phil Wood, editorial director Aaron Wehner, my editor Veronica Randall, and art director Toni Tajima, and all those at Ten Speed Press who supported this second book. I hope it does as well as the first! Thanks for believing in me.

Owning two restaurants and a catering business with close to one hundred employees, there are so many people that make the whole thing work: from the chefs to the managers, to the dishwashers to the line cooks, to the bartenders and waitstaff, the purveyors that have bent over backward for me, the landlords, the trash collectors, the mailwomen. The names and faces change, but the importance of each person in those positions does not. All are needed to keep the doors open and complete a meal service, a wedding, a baby luau, a fundraiser, a wake. I am just the leader of an incredible team of people that keep it all going year after year after year. I thank all of those who have passed through the doors of Hali'imaile General Store, Joe's in Wailea, and Celebrations Catering. You make it happen.

To (in alphabetical order) Allison, Andy, Annalyn, April, Belia, Bubba, Carol, Crystal, Dana, Gabe, Jesse, John, Kalen, Kyle, Meagan, Michael, Michelle, Tim x 2, Wendy, and all those whose names are not here (sorry!) but you are there and you are awesome. You make me proud.

To Tom, Sharon, and your staff, you make me understand the meaning of "no man is an island."

To Mike, Paula (sixteen years and counting), Frieda, John, Joan (twenty years and counting), you keep catering, catering!

To Jackie, I am glad you can count!

To Henry, I hear you are retiring soon. Over my dead body!

To Rebecca, remember, I only have a sushi waitress position open! You are truly my savior!!

To my incredible, fabulous, understanding husband, after twenty-eight years you rock my world. Your "being kind rather than right" philosophy has impacted us and made us love each other more than I thought we could. I absolutely will love you forever and ever.

To all of those people who have touched my life, you make me who I am. You all make an imprint on my life's DNA. I hope I can continue to make you proud. I love you all.

And, no, there is no crab dip recipe in this book either!

Introduction

FAMILY SUPPERS were a part of every day life when I was growing up in Dallas, Texas. My parents, my brother, sister, and I would gather around the table in the evening and recount the day's events and activities while filling our tummies with basic, simple foods.

My mother wasn't a particularly great cook, but she did manage to put meals on the table every day. I'm not sure how she did it, but I do remember what she did: each day of the week, every week, year after year, was a specific type of food with some occasional surprises thrown in.

Sundays were about brunch and food from the deli, like lox and bagels and corned beef. I remember Dad filleting smoked whitefish as we anxiously anticipated that first delicious bite. On Sunday nights, the grill was king: chicken, steaks, burgers, ribs, jumbo prawns. During the summer months, we always hung out around the swimming pool and we'd invite all our friends over. Being the Jewish mother, my mom would always make sure everyone was fed with something she cooked or ordered in, like burgers from the newly opened Burger King, pizza, or great fried chicken from Youngblood's, which, to this day, is my favorite double-battered fried chicken. We never lacked for an abundance of food.

Mondays were chop-suey days that utilized leftovers from the weekend. Mom might take some grilled beef or chicken from Sunday night's barbecue and stir-fry it with some leftover vegetables. Or we might just have a bunch of leftovers, a mix of this and that and a little more of this—a mix of whatever happened to be in the refrigerator.

Fish was usually served on Tuesdays, not usually fresh fish but frozen fish, being rather landlocked in Dallas. My mother, like most home cooks of the day, cooked fish well done. Fillet of sole was cooked at 350 degrees F for an hour, or until crispy around the edges. I usually left the house when lobsters were boiled to death because I couldn't stand the smell. It was way-overcooked-fish day at my house, a day when I tried my best to go to a friend's house for dinner.

One of my favorite dishes was my mother's tuna-noodle casserole. She made it with the usual mushrooms, mushroom soup, peas, and tuna fish, all from cans, with potato chips on the top. My mother grew up on a farm, so canned and frozen foods were a treat for her to use. Other casseroles that appeared on Wednesdays would combine leftover brisket with canned corn and chiles, Velveeta cheese, and Rotel tomatoes—or beef with broccoli and canned cheddar-cheese soup. I still love casseroles—the marrying of ingredients held together by a sauce—but I use ingredients that are fresh and homemade, like just-caught tuna, free-range chicken, corn, tomatoes, artichokes, fennel, fresh herbs, and homemade stocks and sauces.

Our favorite day of the week was Thursday—where's-the-beef day. Thick sirloin steaks were a favorite; at our house, it was one giant piece of sirloin for each member of the family (!) served up with stuffed baked or mashed potatoes. Lamb and pork were served on this day too. My mother would shop for weeks to find the perfect meaty lamb shanks. My father could eat three or four with no problem. Vegetables came from the convenience of the "can"—Jolly Green Giant asparagus and Le Sueur peas.

Rotisserie chicken was one of my mother's best meals, plump roasters slowly turned on a tabletop

rotisserie, basted with its own juices. The meat was so succulent and tasty. Even when the kids were gone, she cooked several chickens every Friday night, just in case anyone would stop by and need to eat. Of course the leftovers were terrific too, and were turned into pot pies, quesadillas, casseroles, and other homey dishes.

Just about anything could pop up on the dinner table on Saturday night—my mom never knew who would be home, especially as we teenagers attended to our social lives. Sometimes she'd make a soup or a main course salad; a pasta dish might emerge with leftover chicken from the night before. Dinner was always a surprise, but we knew it was always there and that there was enough to have six or eight friends show up hungry. My house was well known for its full-of-food-at-all-times fridge. Friends would walk in the backdoor and head straight to the fridge; they knew my mother loved that they felt comfortable enough to raid the fridge anytime.

Now, years later, I can appreciate my mother's efforts, having cooked for a family of five every night. While I cook on a larger scale, overseeing preparations for a few hundred for dinner every night, I can see the wisdom of her schedule of menus and relish the memories of the many simple meals she prepared for our family.

When I moved to Maui almost thirty years ago, family became an even more precious aspect of my life. Not only did I inherit a family when I married my husband, Joe, I was also introduced to the concept of 'ohana, or family, in the Hawaiian sense. Culturally the people of Hawai'i, who come from all corners of the earth, hold family and family values in high esteem. So family gatherings—daily, weekly, or when there is an occasion to celebrate—are a part of everyday life. And of course each family gathering is centered around food, another important aspect of Hawai'i's culture.

In the past two decades, there has been a tremendous renaissance in the food of Hawai'i: farmers are producing incredible fruits and vegetables, fish has become the star of the plate, and there's a lot of focus on freshness and quality. My peers in the restaurant world are creating wonderful food, and together we've garnered attention for Hawai'i's regional cuisine, a cuisine that mirrors the many ethnic groups that live here and that makes Hawai'i a food lover's paradise.

In this cookbook, I hope that some of my food will become the bonding agent for your family gatherings. There's nothing more fun and satisfying to me than to sit down with my family over food I have cooked or that I've cooked together with my family. In this fast-paced and overcrowded-schedules world, family time—where the whole family sits down to a home-cooked meal—has become a lost art. It's so sad, because the satisfaction one gets from presenting a home-cooked meal is priceless. Take some time to renew your cooking skills and cook, cook, cook.

I know that as a restaurant chef, dishes sometimes get complicated and have many parts. The recipes in this book are meant to be prepared by the home cook. If you always follow my basic rule of prepping all your ingredients before you start to cook, the making of the dish becomes fairly simple. Some recipes may have more ingredients than you are used to using, but don't let that scare you. Think of the preparation of each of the many recipes as an adventure. If you like to cook, you will love my recipes, and once you get used to the process, you will make them over and over. I believe in giving you recipes that you can execute yourself.

While I don't follow my mother's rule of fish Tuesdays, casserole Wednesdays, beef Thursdays, and so on in my restaurant, the protein is the key element of a dish. So I've organized this cookbook around the

Family and food are a natural combination and it's the essence of what happens at Hali'imaile General Store, day in and day out. With the help of my hardworking and dedicated staff, I am able to provide the food and the tables around which families come together to dine. It's here where birthdays, engagements, weddings, anniversaries, graduations, special holidays, and just simple family get-togethers are celebrated with the sharing of a meal. Many times food is ordered and passed around to share, each person taking a bite from another's plate. The focal point is the food, but the bond it creates is about the family.

prime protein ingredients and days of the week. I hope that you'll find this a useful way to begin your family-cooking adventures. Even though some dishes are appetizers, soups, or salads, each can become an entrée, especially on those busy days when one-dish meals are your plan.

The recipes serve four, six, eight, or sometimes more. Halve a recipe or double it, depending on how many people you'll be serving. The more the merrier I say, when it comes to cooking up a pot of chili or a meatloaf; you can always have a chop-suey night of leftovers or freeze extras for another day.

I am all for getting the kids in the kitchen to help prepare meals. It's what I did as a child and what my children did when they grew up. When kids get their hands on food and can experience what it takes to get a meal on the table, they'll no doubt enjoy eating the meal itself and grow up with an appreciation for the effort it takes to make food. Besides, teaching kids to cook prepares them for their lives as adults by giving them some basic skills to fend for themselves.

No matter the day of the week or the occasion to celebrate, let food become the bond for your family. Over the years at Hali'imaile General Store, people have walked through the door to share a meal and then leave the table satisfied and fulfilled with more than just food. For me, Hali'imaile General Store is my home—I spend more time here than at home—and the people who walk through the door have become like family. I love sharing my food, just as my mother shared her food with our family, bonding us forever.

Beverly Gannon
Hali'imaile General Store
Joe's in Wailea
Celebrations Catering

Bev's Basics

I'M NOT AT ALL OPPOSED to using prepared foods that will save you time and effort. Store-bought rotisserie chicken, for example, can become a key ingredient for a great casserole or quesadilla with the addition of fresh embellishments and tasty sauces. While making everything from scratch can't be beat, it's sometimes just not possible within today's busy schedules and lives.

That said, it's both efficient and cost effective to stock your cupboards and fridge with a few essentials that can be prepared ahead of time and stored for later use. Stocks and demi-glaces are easy to make, add more flavor than you can imagine, and are good for the environment because they utilize ingredients that would otherwise be thrown out. Premixed spices and dipping sauces can even elevate everyday fare to favorite party dishes.

Good food, like everything else we do, requires some planning and effort, but the delicious results are well worth it.

Bev's Basics

pantry essentials

Butter: I always use unsalted butter in cooking and baking so that I can control the amount of salt in a preparation. Use unsalted butter in all recipes.

Flour: Use all-purpose flour in all recipes unless otherwise noted.

Oil: In my restaurants, I use a blend of canola and olive oils for sautéing, frying, and general cooking. For general home cooking, I recommend canola oil; use it in all my recipes unless a recipe specifies a different oil. In some instances, I like to use peanut oil because it can be heated to a higher temperature. But because of allergic reactions, I do not use it in my restaurants anymore. If you are not allergic to peanut oil, by all means use it, especially when deep-frying.

Salt: I always use kosher salt in my kitchens and on my tables; all the recipes in this book are based on kosher salt. It's a little less salty than regular table salt, so adjust accordingly: 1 teaspoon of kosher salt equals $1/2$ teaspoon of table salt.

Wine: In cooking, I always use a wine that I would drink. You don't have to use an expensive or estate wine; a generic chardonnay for white, cabernet sauvignon or merlot for red, or a ruby red port will do. Wines have to taste good for a dish to taste good.

fish stock

If you make your own fish stock for use in soups, the soup will be that much more flavorful. When you make fish stock, use fresh fish heads and meaty bones from mild-flavored white fish. Blood, gills, and viscera should be removed; rinse all heads and bones well before proceeding. Salmon and other oily fish are not recommended unless you are using the stock to complement those fish. Fish stock can be made ahead and frozen for later use.

If you want a really rich and flavorful sauce, make the recipe below once, strain it, and add enough water to make 6 cups of stock. Then repeat the recipe, adding all the ingredients to the stock that has already been made.

2	**pounds fish heads and bones**
1	**large onion, quartered**
1	**carrot, peeled and cut into chunks**
1	**leek, cleaned and sliced**
1	**clove garlic, peeled and crushed**
2	**sprigs parsley**
1	**bay leaf**
12	**whole black peppercorns**
1	**cup white wine**
6	**cups water or enough to cover**
Salt	

1. Preheat the oven to 350 degrees F.

2. Place the fish heads and bones on a baking sheet. Place in the oven and roast for about 30 minutes, until lightly browned.

3. Transfer the fish heads and bones to a large stockpot, scraping any bits from the baking sheet. Add all the other ingredients except the salt to the stockpot and set over medium heat. Bring to a boil, reduce the heat, and simmer gently for about 30 minutes. Strain into a clean pot. Add salt. Cool and refrigerate until ready to use, or freeze for later use.

Makes about 1 ¹/₂ quarts

veal stock/demi-glace

Veal stock is one of the basics of classic cooking, adding great depth of flavor and substance to a dish. Veal stock becomes demi-glace simply by reducing unseasoned stock on the stovetop for several hours. If you cannot find veal bones, use beef bones, which will give you a stronger-flavored stock. Stock and demi-glace can be made and stored in the freezer.

3 to 4 pounds veal bones

2   **carrots, peeled and cut into 2-inch pieces**

2   **stalks celery, cut into 2-inch pieces**

1   **large onion, peeled and quartered**

2   **leeks, white part only, cut into 2-inch pieces**

2   **cloves garlic**

1   **bay leaf**

1   **teaspoon whole black peppercorns**

4   **sprigs parsley**

1   **sprig fresh thyme**

Salt

Freshly ground pepper

1. Preheat oven to 400 degrees F.

2. Place the veal bones in a roasting pan. Roast the bones for 45 to 60 minutes, until the bones are dark brown. Transfer the bones to a large stockpot. Add water to the roasting pan and scrape any brown bits from the pan; transfer this liquid to the stockpot.

3. Add the carrots, celery, onion, leeks, and garlic to the stockpot. Place the bay leaf, peppercorns, parsley, and thyme in a piece of cheesecloth and tie into a bundle. Place the herb bundle in the stockpot. Add enough water to generously cover all the ingredients.

4. Place the pot over medium-high heat and bring to a boil. Skim the surface of any scum and oil as it appears. Once the liquid comes to a boil, decrease the heat and simmer for 5 to 6 hours, adding more water if needed to keep all the ingredients covered.

5. Remove the bones and vegetables from the stockpot with a slotted spoon and discard. Carefully pour the liquid through a fine mesh strainer into another stockpot. Cool the stock and refrigerate overnight.

6. Remove any solid fat from the stock. Reheat the stock to use it, seasoning it with salt and pepper. Or stock can be portioned into containers and frozen for future use.

7. To make demi-glace, place the stockpot over medium-high heat and bring to a boil. Decrease the heat to medium and continue to simmer until the stock has reduced to a thick liquid that will coat the back of a spoon. Cool and refrigerate. Demi-glace will be firm and can be cut into 1/4- or 1/2-cup portions and frozen for later use.

Makes about 1 quart

blackening spice mix

2	cups paprika
8	tablespoons chili powder
1	tablespoon salt
2	teaspoons fennel seeds
2	teaspoons cumin seeds
2	teaspoons onion powder
2	teaspoons cayenne pepper
2	teaspoons white pepper
2	teaspoons black pepper
2	teaspoons garlic powder
2	teaspoons red pepper flakes
2	tablespoons dry basil
2	tablespoons dry oregano
2	tablespoons dill weed

1. To make the spice mix, combine all the ingredients in a large mixing bowl and mix well. Store spice mix in an airtight container.

Makes about 3 cups

chinese five-spice powder

1	cinnamon stick, about 3 inches in length
8	whole cloves
1	whole star anise
1	teaspoon fennel seeds
25	Szechuan peppercorns

1. Break the cinnamon stick into pieces. Place all the spices in a spice grinder and grind to a fine powder. Store in an airtight jar for up to 2 months.

Makes about 2 tablespoons

chive oil

1   cup olive oil

1   cup chopped fresh chives

1. In a blender, place the olive oil and the chives. On high speed, blend the mixture for 1 minute. Pour into a bowl and let steep for 2 to 3 hours. With a fine mesh strainer, strain the oil into a jar. Discard the solids. Cover and refrigerate for up to 2 weeks.

Makes about 1 cup

hali'imaile barbecue sauce

2   tablespoons margarine

2   onions, chopped

3   cups ketchup

1¹/₂ cups canned red chile sauce

¹/₂   cup cider vinegar

¹/₂   cup firmly packed brown sugar

¹/₃   cup yellow mustard (any brand)

¹/₃   cup dark molasses

2   teaspoons cayenne pepper

¹/₃   cup Worcestershire sauce

2   teaspoons liquid smoke

Juice of ¹/₂ lemon

Juice of ¹/₂ lime

Juice of ¹/₂ orange

Salt

Freshly ground black pepper

1. To prepare the sauce, in a heavy saucepan, melt the margarine over medium heat. Add the onions and sauté for 5 to 6 minutes, until translucent. Add all the remaining ingredients, stir to blend, and bring to a boil. Decrease the heat and simmer, uncovered, for 2 hours, until thick and reddish brown.

Makes about 6 cups

mango-chile dipping sauce

1   **large ripe mango**

3   **cups rice vinegar**

4   **cups sugar**

½   **cup seeded and finely diced red bell pepper**

½   **cup finely diced red onion**

1   **tablespoon chopped fresh ginger**

1   **tablespoon chopped fresh cilantro**

1   **tablespoon chopped fresh mint**

1   **teaspoon sambal oelek (Indonesian chile sauce)**

1. Peel the mango and remove the flesh from the seed and dice. Place the mango in a food processor or blender and purée, adding a small amount of water if necessary for smoothness. Measure ¾ cup of purée. Leftover mango purée can be stored in an airtight container in the refrigerator for up to 2 weeks or frozen for later use.

2. To prepare the sauce, combine the vinegar and sugar in a saucepan over medium-high heat and bring to a boil. Stir to dissolve the sugar and continue to cook for 35 to 40 minutes, until the mixture is reduced and syrupy. Add the bell pepper, onion, ginger, cilantro, mint, and sambal oelek to the sugar syrup. Stir well, remove from the heat, and cool. Stir in the mango purée.

Makes about 4 cups

Brunch

I LOVE SUNDAY BRUNCH. In our family, Sunday brunch was always a big spread, starting around 11 A.M. or noon. It was probably one of the few breakfasts where we sat down and ate as a family. We never knew who would be there besides us; it was usually ten or twelve people sitting around the dining table.

Sunday brunch was a Jewish traditional meal. It was based on deli food: lox and bagels, corned beef, salami, tomatoes and onions, cheeses, pickled herring, baked salmon (still one of my favorite things to eat), and plates of scrambled eggs (rarely were there omelets).

My father would get big smoked whitefish, one to two pounds of fish, and he would meticulously skin it, bone it, and serve it to us. My mother made the best chopped liver and occasionally she'd make tongue, cooked in a pressure cooker, something she used a lot. Once in a while, she would make fried chicken liver omelets with caramelized onions that we'd eat with a ton of ketchup. There would be rye bread, twisted egg bread, or sometimes Mom would make French toast with challah. A crunchy chopped salad of radishes, cucumbers, celery, and cabbage would be on the table. Tomato juice was always served along with orange juice and milk.

I used to love to do Sunday brunch at Hali'imaile General Store. Omelets, huevos rancheros, eggs Benedict, and other brunchy items won us awards for Sunday brunch. But it became so difficult to open every day at lunchtime; we just needed a break. We still do Sunday brunch for special days like Easter and Mother's Day. And once in a while, I'll cook up a favorite dish or two for Joe and the family to enjoy. It's a delicious tradition that I love.

Brunch

lox, eggs, and onions

As I grew up, this was my favorite way to eat eggs. I was always first in the kitchen with a bowl when my mother made these eggs. One of her secrets was to caramelize the onions until they were really soft and brown and really good. In my early years on Maui, I would order smoked fish from Alan at Barney Greengrass, a Jewish deli in New York, and he would always stick a container of these eggs in my order box.

12   eggs

Salt

Freshly ground white pepper

¼   cup heavy cream

4   tablespoons butter

1   cup thinly sliced onion

½   pound cold-smoked salmon, julienned

1   tablespoon finely chopped fresh chives

1. To prepare the eggs, in a large mixing bowl, crack the eggs. Beat the eggs with a whisk. Season with salt and pepper. Add the cream and mix well.

2. To prepare the onions, in a large nonstick sauté pan over medium heat, melt the butter. Add the onions and cook, stirring occasionally, until the onions take on a caramel color, about 10 to 12 minutes. Add the eggs to the pan and with a rubber spatula stir together the eggs and onions until the eggs are loosely cooked. Add the salmon and cook until the eggs are just cooked through. Transfer to a serving dish. Sprinkle with the chives and serve immediately.

Serves 6

ingredient note: *Cold-smoked salmon, or lox, is a kind of smoked salmon that has been first soaked in a brine, then cold smoked at about 70 to 90 degrees F. It has a "raw" quality unlike hot-smoked salmon. Geographic references like Nova, Nova Scotia, Scotch, Danish, and Irish added to the word "smoked" indicates a cold-smoked salmon.*

mom's chopped chicken livers

I've been eating this dish since I was a child; my mother made it every Friday night, we would eat it through the weekend, and it ended up on a piece of toast on Sunday. My mother's chopped chicken livers were especially good because she used chicken fat that she rendered herself. My recipe uses butter, adding that silky texture that makes this better than any duck liver pâté with cognac.

1	pound chicken livers
¹⁄₂	cup (16 tablespoons) butter, at room temperature
3	tablespoons chicken stock
1	cup finely diced onions
3	eggs, hard cooked and coarsely chopped
1	teaspoon dried thyme

Salt

Finely ground black pepper

1. In a colander, rinse the chicken livers with cold water. Drain, transfer to paper towels, and pat dry.

2. In a large sauté pan over medium heat, melt 2 tablespoons of the butter. Add the livers to the pan and sauté for about 5 minutes, or until the livers are just cooked through. Do not overcook! Transfer the livers to a large bowl.

3. Add 1 tablespoon of the chicken stock to the sauté pan and deglaze the pan, using a rubber spatula to scrape and remove all bits of cooked liver. Transfer the liquid and bits to the bowl.

4. Place the sauté pan back on the heat and add 2 tablespoons of butter. Add the onions and cook until the onions are caramelized and slightly crispy. Transfer the onions to the bowl with the livers. Add the remaining 2 tablespoons of chicken stock to the pan and deglaze it; continue to cook the stock until it is reduced by half. Transfer this liquid to the bowl with the livers.

5. Add the eggs and thyme to the livers. Season with salt and pepper and mix well. Add the remaining 12 tablespoons of butter to the chicken liver mixture. Transfer half of the liver mixture to a food processor outfitted with a metal blade. Pulse 3 to 4 times to coarsely blend the ingredients together. Transfer to a clean bowl. Process the remaining liver mixture. With a rubber spatula, blend the mixture together well. Taste and adjust the seasoning.

6. Line a mold or a bowl with plastic wrap and pour in the liver mixture. Cover with plastic wrap and press down to compress the mixture. Refrigerate for 2 hours to set. Serve with crackers.

Serves 8

fresh and smoked salmon cakes
with poached eggs and horseradish hollandaise

I went salmon fishing in Alaska a few years ago to film a segment of *Let's Go Fishing* and came back with 150 pounds of fresh wild salmon for the restaurants. I wanted to make a good salmon cake and came up with this recipe that also includes smoked salmon. The key to my salmon cake is that the salmon is raw; when you sauté the cakes, the fresh salmon is just cooked through and you don't overcook the smoked salmon.

SALMON CAKES

1/2   **pound fresh wild salmon, cut into 1/4-inch dice**

1/4   **pound cold-smoked salmon, cut into 1-inch strips**

1/4   **cup finely diced celery**

1/4   **cup finely diced red onion**

3   **tablespoons thinly sliced green onions**

2   **tablespoons finely chopped capers**

2   **tablespoons finely chopped fresh dill**

1   **cup panko (Japanese breadcrumbs)**

3   **egg yolks**

1/4   **cup mayonnaise**

Salt

Freshly ground black pepper

HORSERADISH HOLLANDAISE

8   **egg yolks**

1 1/2 **tablespoons freshly squeezed lemon juice**

1   **cup butter, melted**

1   **tablespoon white horseradish**

Salt

POACHED EGGS

3   **tablespoons white vinegar**

12   **eggs**

Fresh dill sprigs, for garnish

1. To prepare the salmon cakes, place the fresh and smoked salmon in a large mixing bowl. Add the celery, red onion, green onions, capers, dill and 3 tablespoons of the panko. Mix together lightly. Add the egg yolks and mayonnaise. Season with salt and pepper and mix well. Cover and refrigerate for 30 minutes.

2. Place the remaining panko in a shallow dish. Divide the salmon mixture into 12 equal-size portions, about 3 ounces each. Shape each portion into a flat disk, about 1/2-inch thick. Coat each disk with the panko, pressing so that the panko sticks to the salmon cake. Line a baking sheet with waxed paper. Place the salmon cakes on the baking sheet. Refrigerate for at least 1 hour to set the cakes.

3. To prepare the sauce, fill a 2-quart saucepan halfway with water. Over high heat, bring the water to a boil, then decrease the heat so the water simmers. In a medium stainless steel bowl with a wire whisk, beat the egg yolks and lemon juice until the yolks thicken to a ribbon. Place the bowl over the simmering water and continually whisk the eggs for two minutes. Slowly drizzle in the melted butter, whisking constantly. The sauce will thicken. Add the horseradish and mix well. Season with salt. Pour the sauce into a thermos. Cover and set aside until ready to use.

4. Preheat the oven to 200 degrees F, or use a warming drawer set on low.

5. In a large sauté pan over medium-high heat, sauté the salmon cakes in batches about 2 minutes on each side until golden brown. Transfer to a baking sheet and keep warm in the oven.

6. To prepare the eggs, fill a large bowl or pan of warm water. Fill a medium-size deep skillet or shallow saucepan with 2 to 3 inches of water.

continued on page 24

leftovers? If there are any salmon cakes left, reheat them and serve them with a fresh green salad that includes cucumbers, tomatoes, and feta cheese. Or serve salmon cakes alongside a grilled flank steak.

Bring the water to a boil over high heat, then decrease the heat so that the water simmers. Add the vinegar. Using 2 small bowls, crack an egg into each bowl. Using a slotted spoon, stir the simmering water to make it swirl. Drop an egg into the center of the swirling water. Using the slotted spoon, help the egg white to swirl around the yolk. Repeat with the second egg. Cook the eggs for about 3 minutes for soft yolks. Using the slotted spoon, transfer the eggs to the pan with the warm water. Repeat the process until all the eggs are cooked.

7. Remove the salmon cakes from the oven and place two cakes in the center of a plate. Using a slotted spoon remove and drain the poached eggs and place one on top of each cake. Pour horseradish hollandaise over each egg. Garnish with fresh dill sprig. Serve immediately.

Serves 6

hali'imaile huevos rancheros

This used to be one of the most popular dishes on our menu when we served brunch at Hali'imaile General Store. When we'd do special holiday brunches, we'd serve it again, wondering why we didn't put it on the menu for lunch—so I just did! Most ranchero sauces are smooth, but this one is chunky, making it a dish of substance.

RANCHERO SAUCE

2	tablespoons olive oil
1	cup coarsely chopped onions
1¹/₂	cups ¹/₂-inch slices zucchini, quartered
¹/₂	cup thinly sliced celery
1	cup coarsely chopped red bell pepper
4	cloves garlic, minced
3	cups canned crushed tomatoes
1	tablespoon tomato paste
1	tablespoon ground cumin
1	tablespoon chile powder
2	teaspoons Tabasco
¹/₂	cup sliced black olives
12	corn tortillas
¹/₂	cup shredded sharp Cheddar cheese
¹/₂	cup shredded Monterey Jack cheese
4	tablespoons butter
12	eggs
¹/₄	cup chopped fresh cilantro

1. To prepare the sauce, in a large sauté pan over medium-high heat, add the olive oil. Add the onions and cook for 2 minutes. Add the zucchini and the celery and cook for 1 minute. Add the red peppers and cook for 2 minutes, stirring frequently. Add the garlic and stir. Add the tomatoes, tomato paste, cumin, chile powder, and Tabasco. Bring the mixture to a boil, decrease the heat to a simmer and cook, uncovered, for 8 to 10 minutes, or until the sauce thickens but the vegetables are still reasonably firm. Add the olives and stir. Remove from the heat and keep warm.

2. Preheat the oven to 350 degrees F. Wrap the tortillas in aluminum foil and heat in the oven for 10 minutes.

3. In a small bowl, mix together the cheeses.

4. To prepare the eggs, in a 6-inch nonstick pan over medium-high heat, add 2 teaspoons of the butter. Crack 2 eggs into a small bowl. Pour the eggs into the pan and cook until the whites are set and the yolks are soft. Repeat with all the eggs.

5. Place 2 tortillas on a plate. Cover with ¹/₃ cup of the sauce. Sprinkle with the mixed cheeses. Top with 2 fried eggs. Sprinkle with cilantro and serve.

Serves 6

leftovers? Ranchero sauce can be used to top a grilled chicken breast or piece of fish. Use it in a burrito with leftover Beef Brisket (page 119) or with black beans and cheese.

pimento cheese omelet

Once I take a bite of this homemade Pimento Cheese, I have a hard time not eating a bowl of it. That's why this recipe is larger than you need for the six omelets you'll make. Believe me, if you don't get the Pimento Cheese into the omelets quickly, everyone will start eating it and it will be gone! Be sure to use a sharp or extra-sharp cheese for this recipe.

PIMENTO CHEESE

3   hard-cooked eggs, coarsely grated

¹/₄   cup finely grated onion

16   ounces canned pimentos with juice

2   cups mayonnaise

3   tablespoons Colman's dry mustard

1¹/₂   teaspoons Worcestershire sauce

2   teaspoons salt

2   pounds sharp yellow Cheddar cheese, grated

OMELET

18   eggs

Salt

Freshly ground black pepper

4   tablespoons butter

1. To prepare the pimento cheese, in a large mixing bowl with a spatula, blend together the hard-cooked eggs, onion, pimentos, mayonnaise, mustard, Worcestershire sauce, and salt. Add the cheese in handfuls and mix the wet ingredients into the cheese without mashing down the cheese. Make sure all the ingredients are well combined. Cover and refrigerate until ready to use.

2. To prepare the omelet, break 3 eggs into a small mixing bowl. Season with salt and pepper and beat with a whisk until well blended.

3. In a nonstick 8-inch omelet pan over medium-high heat, melt 2 teaspoons of the butter. Pour in the beaten eggs. Let the eggs set. When the edges are set, using a rubber spatula, push one edge of the omelet toward the middle and tilt the pan, allowing the uncooked egg to pour into the empty space. Tilt the pan in the opposite direction and move the other edge to the center of the pan, allowing the rest of the uncooked egg to fill the empty space. Cook the eggs for another 2 minutes. Place 2 tablespoons of the cheese filling on one half of the omelet. With a plate near the pan, slide the side of the omelet with the cheese onto the plate, then, with a twist of the wrist, flip the other half of the omelet over the cheese mixture. Repeat with the remaining eggs and serve immediately.

Serves 6

leftovers? You will have lots of leftover pimento cheese filling. It stores well, covered, in the refrigerator for up to 3 weeks. Spread it on crackers, make grilled pimento cheese sandwiches. Fill baked phyllo cups or pastry shells with this mixture to serve for hors d'oeuvres. No matter how much you make, it will disappear fast!

baked sausage casserole
with chunky fresh tomato sauce

This is the breakfast casserole I would make when I knew we were having a group of teenagers spend the night. I'd wake up in the morning, turn on the oven, and look in the refrigerator for anything I could mix with eggs and cheese to combine into a hearty breakfast for hungry teens. They thought this was gourmet cooking! Instead of Italian sausage, you can use shrimp, bacon, ham, leftover lamb, chicken, turkey, or vegetables—whatever you happen to have.

CASSEROLE

1	pound loaf sourdough bread, cut into 1/2-inch cubes
1	pound russet potatoes, peeled and cut into 1/2-inch cubes
1	pound spicy Italian sausage, casings removed and coarsely crumbled
2	tablespoons butter
2	cups thinly sliced red bell pepper
1/4	cup finely chopped shallots
1/2	teaspoon salt, plus additional salt
1/4	teaspoon freshly ground black pepper, plus additional pepper
2	tablespoons minced fresh chives
2	tablespoons minced fresh oregano
3	cups grated smoked Gouda cheese
6	eggs
3	cups half-and-half
2	tablespoons Dijon-style mustard
2	cups Chunky Fresh Tomato Sauce (recipe follows)

1. Preheat the oven to 400 degrees F.

2. Grease a 9 by 13-inch deep casserole dish. Set aside.

3. To prepare the casserole, place the bread on a baking sheet and place in the oven. Bake until lightly golden brown, about 12 minutes. Remove and set aside to cool.

4. In a large pot of salted water over high heat, cook the potatoes until barely cooked through, about 5 minutes. Drain the potatoes.

5. In a large skillet over medium-high heat, add the sausage and cook, breaking up the sausage with a wooden spoon. When the sausage is browned and cooked through, about 8 to 10 minutes, transfer it to a paper towel-lined plate to drain the excess oil. Transfer to a large bowl. Reserve the drippings.

6. In the same sauté pan over medium-high heat, add 1 tablespoon of the butter and 1 tablespoon of the sausage drippings. Add the red peppers and sauté until limp and lightly browned, about 5 to 7 minutes. Transfer to the bowl with the sausage.

7. In the same sauté pan, melt the remaining 1 tablespoon of butter with 1 tablespoon of the sausage drippings. Add the potatoes and cook until the potatoes are lightly browned and tender, stirring occasionally. Add the shallots and sauté until soft, about 2 minutes. Transfer the potatoes and shallots to the bowl with the sausage and peppers. Season with salt and pepper.

8. Add the chives, oregano, and Gouda and mix well. Add the bread and mix well.

9. Transfer the mixture to the prepared casserole dish.

10. In a large bowl with a wire whisk, blend together the eggs, half-and-half, mustard, 1/2 teaspoon salt, and 1/4 teaspoon pepper. Pour the egg mixture over the sausage mixture. Cover and refrigerate for 2 to 3 hours, until the bread completely soaks up the liquid, occasionally pressing the bread into the custard. (This dish can be made a day ahead. Bring to room temperature 30 minutes before baking.)

11. Preheat the oven to 350 degrees F.

12. To make the tomato sauce, in a medium saucepan over medium heat, add the olive oil. When it's hot, add the onions, carrots, celery, and garlic and sauté, stirring frequently, until the ingredients are wilted, about 4 to 5 minutes. Add the canned, fresh, and puréed tomatoes and stir to blend. Add the oregano and basil and cook, uncovered, for 30 to 40 minutes, stirring occasionally, until the sauce thickens. Season with salt and pepper. Add sugar, if needed.

13. Bake the casserole, uncovered, until the custard is set, about 45 to 50 minutes. Remove from the oven, cool for a few minutes, then cut into squares. Serve with the tomato sauce.

Serves 8

CHUNKY FRESH TOMATO SAUCE

3	tablespoons olive oil
1/2	cup finely diced onions
1/2	cup peeled and finely diced carrots
1/2	cup finely diced celery
2	teaspoons finely minced garlic cloves
4	cups canned whole peeled tomatoes
3	cups coarsely chopped ripe, seeded fresh tomatoes
2	cups canned tomato purée
1	tablespoon fresh oregano leaves
1	tablespoon chopped fresh basil

Salt

Freshly ground black pepper

1	teaspoon sugar

leftovers? Serve this tomatoey sauce over pasta, with or without meatballs, with freshly grated Parmigiano-Reggiano. Or top grilled chicken breasts and vegetables with this sauce. Freeze leftovers for another night's great meal; it's always good to have this sauce around for an instant meal or condiment.

the ultimate french toast

The key to a good French toast is to make sure the bread is really soaked in the milk and egg mixture. That's what you do when you make this recipe, probably one of the most decadent French toasts you can make. Once you have tried this recipe, all other French toast pales in comparison.

1   quart heavy whipping cream

¹/₂ vanilla bean, split

³/₄ cup, plus 2 tablespoons sugar

8   egg yolks

1   (2-pound) loaf egg bread, sliced into 1-inch cubes

¹/₄ cup Grand Marnier

2   cups fresh blueberries

Confectioners' sugar, for garnish

1. Use a 2-quart loaf pan. Cut a piece of thick cardboard to fit the top of the loaf pan like a cover. Grease the loaf pan. Set aside.

2. In a 2-quart saucepan, over medium-high heat, place the cream, vanilla bean, and the ³/₄ cup sugar and heat until just up to a boil. Remove from the heat. Pour the mixture through a fine-mesh strainer into a bowl. Set aside to cool. When the cream is cool, add the egg yolks and blend with a whisk.

3. Place a layer of the bread in the bottom of the loaf pan. Ladle 3 to 4 tablespoons of the cream mixture onto the bread. Repeat the process until all the bread is used. Pour the rest of the cream over the bread. Cover the pan with plastic wrap. Top the pan with the cardboard cover, allowing it to rest on top of the bread. Place a weight on top of the cardboard—two soup cans will do—and refrigerate for about 2 hours, or overnight, allowing the bread to completely soak up the cream.

4. Preheat the oven to 350 degrees F.

5. Remove the weight, cardboard, and plastic. Place the loaf pan into another pan filled with water three-quarters of the way up the side of the loaf pan. Place the pan in the oven and bake for 1 to 1¹/₂ hours or until the custard is set. Remove from the oven and set aside to cool. When it is cool, cover and place in the refrigerator.

6. When you are ready to serve, preheat the oven to 350 degrees F.

7. Unmold the bread from the loaf pan and cut into 8 slices. In a large sauté pan over medium-high heat, melt the butter. Add the bread and until golden brown, about 3 minutes on each side. Transfer the bread to an ovenproof pan. Place in the oven to heat the bread through, about 5 minutes.

8. In a medium sauté pan over medium-high heat, add the 2 tablespoons sugar and the Grand Marnier. Light a match and touch it to the Grand Marnier to burn off the alcohol. When the flame subsides, whisk together

continued on page 32

the sugar and Grand Marnier. Decrease the heat to low and add the blueberries. With a wooden spoon, blend together the berries and sugar. Cook until the berries begin to break down, about 5 minutes. Set aside and keep warm.

9. To serve, place a piece of French toast on a plate and spoon the blueberry compote over the toast. Using a fine-mesh sieve, sprinkle the confectioners' sugar over the French toast and blueberry compote.

Serves 8

chicken and caramelized onion crêpes
with mixed mushroom sauce

When I began planning the menus for Hawaiian Airlines, this was one of the first dishes we served. It was such a hit that we include it on our special holiday brunch buffets at Hali'imaile General Store. What I like about this crêpe is that the filling is not just about being creamy—it's about the flavor of the chicken and artichokes with the mushroom sauce adding another layer of flavor.

11	tablespoons butter
2	cups thinly sliced onions
1	cup chopped, frozen artichoke hearts
Salt	
Freshly ground black pepper	
1/2	cup fresh corn kernels
2	teaspoons freshly squeezed lime juice
3	cups 1/2-inch cubes Roasted Chicken (page 147)
3	tablespoons thinly sliced green onions
3	tablespoons finely chopped fresh tarragon
1/2	cup grated Asiago cheese

1. Preheat the oven to 350 degrees F.

2. Lightly grease a large, shallow baking dish that will hold the 12 rolled crêpes. Set aside.

3. To prepare the filling, in a medium sauté pan over medium-high heat, melt 3 tablespoons of the butter. Add the onions and cook, stirring occasionally, until they are golden brown in color and caramelized, about 12 to 15 minutes. Transfer to a large mixing bowl.

4. In the same sauté pan over high heat, add 2 tablespoons of the butter. Add the artichoke hearts and cook for 2 minutes. Season with salt and pepper. Transfer to the bowl with the onions.

5. In the same pan over high heat, add 1 tablespoon of the butter. Add the corn and cook for 1 minute. Add the lime juice and cook another 30 seconds. Transfer to the bowl with the onions and artichokes. When the vegetables are cool, add the chicken and toss together. Add the green onions, 1 tablespoon of the tarragon, and the cheese and mix well. Set aside.

2 cups sliced assorted fresh mushrooms (such as shiitake, cremini, lobster, trumpet, porcini)

2 teaspoons chopped garlic

2 tablespoons chopped shallots

2 cups milk

1 cup chicken stock

3 tablespoons flour

12 Crêpes (page 48, made without chives)

6. To make the sauce, in a large sauté pan over high heat, add 2 tablespoons of the butter. Add the mushrooms and sauté for 4 to 5 minutes. Add the garlic and shallots and sauté until any liquid evaporates, about 1 minute. Remove from the heat and set aside.

7. In a saucepan over low heat, heat the milk and chicken stock.

8. In another saucepan, melt the remaining 3 tablespoons of butter. Add the flour and stir with a wire whisk; cook for 2 minutes, whisking continuously. Remove the pan from the heat and slowly whisk in the milk mixture. Place the pan the back on the heat and cook until the sauce thickens, stirring. Add the mushrooms. Season with salt and pepper and mix well.

9. Place a few crêpes on a clean work surface, lighter side facing up. Place a generous spoonful of chicken filling in the center of each crêpe and roll up. Place the crêpes seam side down in the baking dish by twos, leaving a small space in between each two-crêpe portion. Pour the mushroom sauce over the crêpes, filling the space between double crêpes with sauce. Place the baking dish in the oven. Bake for 25 to 35 minutes, or until the sauce is bubbling on the top. Remove from the oven and sprinkle with remaining 2 tablespoons of tarragon.

Serves 6

leftovers? You will have leftover filling. Toss it with a jar of fire-roasted tomatoes, a pinch of chile pepper flakes, 1/2 cup prepared pesto, and a splash of olive oil. Bring it to a simmer. Toss with cooked bow tie pasta and sprinkle with shredded Asiago cheese.

haliʻimaile really sticky buns

This is a Neiman Marcus memory from my Dallas childhood: we would always get a basket of these when we went there. When I opened Haliʻimaile General Store and served brunch, I wanted a good sticky bun just like the ones I had when I was a child. What sets this recipe apart is lots of pecans and the killer sticky part—Karo syrup.

2	packages active dry yeast
1/2	cup warm water, 110 degrees F
1 1/4	cups buttermilk
2	eggs
3/4	cup, plus 2 tablespoons butter, at room temperature
1/2	cup sugar
2	teaspoons baking powder
2	teaspoons salt
6	cups flour
1 1/2	cups firmly packed dark brown sugar
4	teaspoons cinnamon
1	cup dark Karo syrup
3/4	cup butter, melted
1	cup chopped pecans, toasted
1	cup raisins

1. In a large mixing bowl, dissolve the yeast in warm water. Add the buttermilk, eggs, 1/2 cup of the butter, sugar, baking powder, salt, and 2 1/2 cups of the flour. Blend together using a mixer on low speed for 30 seconds, scraping the sides and bottom of the bowl. Beat for 2 minutes on medium speed. Stir in the remaining flour; the dough should be soft and slightly sticky. Transfer the dough to a lightly floured surface and knead for 5 minutes, or about 200 turns. Cover the dough and let rest for 30 minutes.

2. Divide the dough in half and roll each half into a 12 by 8-inch rectangle. Spread each half with 1 tablespoon of butter.

3. In a small bowl, mix together 3/4 cup of the brown sugar and the cinnamon. Sprinkle each rectangle of dough with the brown sugar mixture. Starting at the widest side, roll up each rectangle. Pinch the seams to seal. Cut each roll into 12 slices.

4. Grease 2 (9-inch) round cake pans. Add 1/2 cup of the Karo syrup to each pan, then add half of the melted butter to each pan. Divide the remaining 3/4 cup of brown sugar and sprinkle over the butter, then sprinkle half of the pecans and raisins into each pan. Place 12 slices of the dough in each pan, leaving spaces between the slices. Let the dough rise until doubled, about 1 to 1 1/2 hours.

5. Preheat the oven to 375 degrees F. Bake the buns for 30 minutes. Remove from the oven. Carefully and immediately invert the pans onto serving plates. Serve warm.

Serves 12

potato pancakes
with sour cream and pineapple compote

The first thing I do when I get to New York City is to head to Carnegie Deli for a pastrami sandwich and potato pancakes with sour cream and applesauce, two of my most favorite things to eat. When I make potato pancakes at home, I like to add a tropical touch since I'm surrounded by pineapple fields. The key to making good potato pancakes is to work fast so that the potatoes don't turn brown.

PINEAPPLE COMPOTE

3   tablespoons butter

3   cups 1/2-inch dice fresh pineapple

1/2 cup fresh pineapple juice from the cut pineapple

1/2 cup golden raisins

1/4 cup dark brown sugar

1/4 cup rum

POTATO PANCAKES

4   small russet or Yukon gold potatoes, peeled

1/2 cup flour

1/2 teaspoon baking powder

2   teaspoons salt

1   tablespoon grated onion

2   large eggs, beaten

1/4 cup canola oil

1/4 cup butter

1   cup sour cream

1. Peel the potatoes and place them in a bowl with cold water. Soak for one hour. While the potatoes soak, prepare the compote.

2. To make the compote, in a large sauté pan over high heat, melt the butter. Add the pineapple and cook until golden brown on all sides, about 5 to 7 minutes. Add the pineapple juice and raisins and cook for 2 minutes. Add the brown sugar and stir, about 2 minutes, until the sugar melts. Add the rum and ignite it to burn off the alcohol. Decrease the heat to medium and cook the mixture until it thickens. Remove from the heat, set aside, and keep warm.

3. To prepare the pancakes, remove the potatoes from the water and dry well with a towel.

4. With a grater over a colander, quickly grate the potatoes. In batches, place the potatoes in a clean towel and wring the towel over the sink to remove excess water from the potatoes. Place the potatoes into a mixing bowl.

5. Add the flour, baking powder, and salt, and toss to mix well. Add the onions and eggs and mix well.

6. Heat a large nonstick sauté pan over medium-high heat. Add the canola oil and butter to the preheated pan. Using a 1/4-cup measure, scoop the potato mixture into the pan and form a pancake. Repeat until the pan is full. Cook the pancakes until golden brown and crispy on both sides, about 4 to 5 minutes on each side. Transfer to a plate and keep warm. Continue making more pancakes.

7. Serve the pancakes with a generous dollop of sour cream and the pineapple compote alongside.

Serves 6

nutty crumble coffee cake

Lulu Mae, one of the housekeepers we had when I was growing up in Dallas, often baked treats like this coffee cake for us. Once this cake came out of the oven and was cool enough to eat, it was gone. The original recipe called for pecans; I changed it to macadamia nuts when I moved to Hawai'i.

CRUMBLE

3/4 cup flour

1 1/8 cups firmly packed dark brown sugar

2 tablespoons cinnamon

3/4 cup butter, chilled and cut into small pieces

1 cup coarsely chopped macadamia nuts, lightly toasted

COFFEE CAKE

3/4 cup butter, at room temperature

1 3/4 cups sugar

3 cups sifted flour

4 teaspoons baking powder

1 teaspoon salt

1 1/8 cup milk

4 large egg whites

1. Preheat the oven to 350 degrees F. Grease a 9 by 13-inch baking pan.

2. To prepare the crumble, in a medium bowl, mix together the flour, brown sugar, and cinnamon. Add the butter to the bowl and, using your fingers, crumble the mixture together until it looks like cake crumbs. Add the nuts and mix well. Cover and refrigerate.

3. To make the cake, in a large mixing bowl, using a hand mixer or wooden spoon, cream together the butter and the sugar until smooth. Sift together the flour, baking powder, and salt. Alternating ingredients, add the milk and the flour mixture to the creamed mixture.

4. In a medium bowl, using a hand mixer or wire whisk, beat the egg whites until stiff. Add one-quarter of the egg whites to the batter and fold in to lighten the batter. Fold in the rest of the egg whites. Pour the batter into the prepared pan.

5. Sprinkle the nut crumble over the batter. Place the cake in the oven for 40 to 50 minutes. Remove from the oven when a cake tester inserted into the center comes out clean. Cool on a wire rack and serve.

Serves 8

ingredient note: *Macadamia nuts were introduced to Hawai'i in the late 1800s from Australia and have been produced commercially since 1948, mostly on the island of Hawai'i. It takes seven years for a macadamia nut tree to produce the buttery crunchy nut that we love to snack on. You can substitute macadamia nuts for just about any nut called for in a recipe to add that touch of the islands.*

Stir-Fries

MY FIRST STIR-FRY was my mom's chop suey, which she made often. It was a meal that used up leftovers, usually beef, to which she added canned bamboo shoots and water chestnuts, soy sauce, celery seeds, and garlic. On top, there was always Chun King chow mein noodles!

As a kid, we used to eat take-out Chinese food a lot too. I always equated that food with stir-frying. But it wasn't until I moved to Hawai'i that I did anything in a wok. Shopping at Ah Fook's in Kahului, I saw all sorts of leafy greens and fresh ginger (which I never saw when I was growing up), and pork and chicken cut into bite-sized pieces ready to cook. I went to Liberty House (now Macy's) and bought an electric wok; I thought I was "wok" cool. I made my very first stir-fry and for the next two to three months, I cooked with that wok using a Chinese cookbook, working my way through all the recipes.

I think there's a misconception that stir-fry dishes have to be Asian in flavor. Stir-fries are really about not overcooking food no matter what the flavorings. Stir-fries are a fast way of cooking a combination of things that are cut into the same size so that they all come out crunchy and tasty. Here's what I've learned about stir-frying.

First of all, you don't have to use a wok, though I prefer them. I eventually bought a real wok—a steel wok—that gives you a better sear on food. A wok also allows you to move everything around, and ingredients are not on direct heat all the time because of the high sides and small bottom surface. I can do stir-fries in a sauté pan, but it's easier in a wok to keep everything moving.

Stir-frying should be done over the highest possible heat setting at home. Use oil that tolerates high heat, like grapeseed or peanut oil. (I no longer use peanut oil in the restaurants because of allergies). Canola oil will do. You don't want to use a lot of oil; a minimum amount of oil will keep foods from sticking to the wok.

All the ingredients in a stir-fry should be cut into bite-sized pieces. Clean out your refrigerator: you can use duck, shrimp, beef, pork, or chicken—it's the one time you can mix just about any protein and vegetable and have it be good together.

Stir-fries are all about when you put ingredients into the wok—things that take the longest time to cook go in first. Meats are seared off first then removed. Vegetable stems and ribs are added first, then the leaves. Keep the food moving around.

When I do stir-fries, I don't put my garlic and ginger in at the beginning. I don't like to worry about them burning when the wok is really hot. I add them when I'm almost done.

There are dry stir-fries and wet stir-fries. In wet stir-fries, you add stock, plum sauce, oyster sauce, or another flavor to make a sauce. Stir-fries go well over rice or noodles, but tortillas, pocket breads, and phyllo cups are great too. However you do it, stir-fries are the perfect food for busy home cooks.

Stir-Fries

minced chicken lettuce wraps

When I lived in New York in the 1970s, I thought I had died and gone to heaven when I ate my first squab in lettuce cups at Uncle Tai's on Lexington Ave. This is my version of the experience. My bet is that you can't eat just one of these lettuce cups filled with this well-seasoned chicken mixture. But that's okay—it's a pretty healthy and nutritious dish that can be part of a finger-food meal or served as an entrée.

2 to 3 heads butter lettuce

2 tablespoons oil

1½ pounds boneless, skinless chicken breasts, cut into ½ by ¼-inch thick pieces

1 cup finely sliced fresh shiitake mushrooms

2 tablespoons finely chopped fresh ginger

2 teaspoons finely chopped garlic

½ cup finely sliced green onions

1 cup finely chopped water chestnuts

¼ cup hoisin sauce (Chinese sweet-spicy sauce)

2 tablespoons plum sauce (Chinese duck sauce)

2 teaspoons rice wine vinegar

¾ cup pine nuts, toasted

2 tablespoons finely chopped cilantro

1. Clean and separate the lettuce leaves. Pick through the leaves, using those that will hold a generous 2 tablespoons of the chicken filling. Place the leaves on a serving platter.

2. Heat a wok over high heat until smoking. Add the oil in a circular motion starting 3 inches up from bottom of the wok. Add the chicken and stir-fry for 1 minute. Add the mushrooms; stir-fry for 30 seconds. Add the ginger, garlic, and green onions and stir-fry for 1 minute. Add the water chestnuts, hoisin sauce, plum sauce, and vinegar and stir-fry for 1 minute. Add the pine nuts and the cilantro. Stir to incorporate. Remove the mixture from the heat and transfer to a bowl.

3. Place 2 generous tablespoons of filling in each lettuce leaf, and roll up to eat.

Serves 6

> ingredient notes: *Hoisin sauce is a reddish-brown mixture of soybeans, garlic, spices, and chile peppers used to flavor meat, poultry, and shellfish in Chinese cookery. It is available in jars and cans in Asian food stores and should be stored in the refrigerator after you open it.*
>
> *Plum sauce, also known as duck sauce, is a Chinese condiment made of plums, apricots, and seasonings. It has a sweet-sour flavor and is excellent with duck.*

lemon-cashew chicken stir-fry

Stir-fry dishes are well suited to airline meals because the flavors and textures are not compromised when the dish is reheated. At home, stir-fry dishes are the quickest meal you can make. And if you have any leftovers, they reheat beautifully for lunch the next day. You could use peanuts in this recipe but because of allergies, I use cashews. Jasmine rice is the perfect accompaniment.

1½	pounds boneless, skinless chicken thighs, cut into julienne strips
½	teaspoon salt
¼	teaspoon freshly ground black pepper
4	tablespoons cornstarch
5	tablespoons oil
½	cup thinly sliced red onion
¾	cup julienned red bell pepper
1	cup halved ¼-inch slices zucchini
1	tablespoon finely minced garlic
1½	tablespoons finely chopped fresh ginger
1	cup chicken stock
2	teaspoons sambal oelek (Indonesian chile sauce)
2	teaspoons lemon zest
3	tablespoons freshly squeezed lemon juice
1	teaspoon sugar
1	cup salted dry-roasted whole cashews
¼	cup chopped fresh cilantro
½	cup chopped green onions

1. In a medium bowl, toss the chicken with the salt and pepper. Add 2 tablespoons of the cornstarch and mix well.

2. In a wok over high heat, add 2 tablespoons of the oil and swirl the oil to coat the pan. When the oil is very hot, add one-third of the chicken and stir-fry for 4 minutes. Transfer the chicken to a large mixing bowl and repeat the process, adding oil as needed, until all the chicken is cooked.

3. In the same wok, add 1 tablespoon of the oil and swirl to coat the wok. Add the onions and stir-fry for 1 minute. Add the red bell peppers and stir-fry for 30 seconds. Add the zucchini, garlic, and ginger and stir-fry for 3 minutes. Turn off the heat and transfer the vegetables to the bowl with the chicken.

4. In a small bowl, mix the remaining 2 tablespoons cornstarch with 4 tablespoons of the chicken stock, blending well. Add the sambal, lemon zest, lemon juice, sugar, and the remaining chicken broth to the cornstarch-stock mixture.

5. Reheat the same wok over high heat. Add the chicken stock mixture and cook for 30 seconds until the sauce begins to thicken. Add the chicken and vegetable mixture and toss together well. Continue to stir-fry until the mixture is heated through, about 2 minutes. Add the cashews, cilantro, and green onions and toss. Transfer to a serving dish and serve immediately.

Serves 6

mom's chop suey

Chop suey was always a mystery when I was growing up: you never knew what meat was going to be in it along with canned everything else. Needless to say, this was not one of my favorite meals. But when I moved to Hawai'i and began cooking with fresh ingredients, chop suey became a favorite one-dish family meal. This is my version of Mom's chop suey, updated with fresh and flavorful ingredients. I like to serve this over fragrant jasmine rice.

1	pound beef sirloin, cut into 2 by ¼-inch pieces
1	teaspoon salt
2	tablespoons cornstarch
7	tablespoons oil
½	cup ¼-inch diagonal-cut celery
½	pound fresh shiitake mushrooms, stems removed and halved
½	cup sliced water chestnuts
½	cup sliced bamboo shoots
¼	cup thin, diagonally sliced green onions
1	cup ½-inch slices baby bok choy
1	cup mung bean sprouts, rinsed
2	garlic cloves, minced
2	tablespoons finely minced fresh ginger
1	tablespoon, plus 2 teaspoons oyster sauce
1	tablespoon soy sauce
¼	cup chicken stock
1	tablespoon sesame seeds, toasted

1. Place the beef in a medium bowl, add the salt and toss together. Sprinkle 1 tablespoon of the cornstarch over the meat and mix to coat.

2. In a wok over high heat, add 2 tablespoons of the oil. Swirl the wok to coat the sides with the oil. Add half of the beef to the wok and stir-fry for 2 minutes. Transfer to a plate. Add 1 additional tablespoon of oil, and stir-fry the remaining beef.

3. Add the remaining 4 tablespoons of oil to the wok and swirl to coat the sides. Add the celery and stir-fry for 2 minutes. Add the mushrooms and stir-fry for 2 minutes. Add the water chestnuts, bamboo shoots, green onions, baby bok choy, bean sprouts, garlic, and ginger and stir-fry for 2 minutes. Add the beef, oyster sauce, and soy sauce.

4. Mix the remaining 1 tablespoon of cornstarch with the stock. Make a well in the center of the ingredients in the wok and pour in the cornstarch mixture. Bring the mixture to a boil and then stir-fry for 1 minute to coat the beef and vegetables. Sprinkle in the toasted sesame seeds. Transfer to a serving bowl and serve immediately.

Serves 6

red curry duck

Whenever I'm on an airplane headed for Thailand, I think about this dish served at the Oriental Hotel in Bangkok. It is truly one of my favorite things to eat. I once tried to get the recipe from the chef, but language was a barrier; I got the basic ingredients and made the rest up. If the heat of the red curry paste is too much for you, pineapple juice and brown sugar will tone it down.

1	Chinese roast duck
1	tablespoon peanut oil
1	cup sliced onions
3	tablespoons Thai red curry paste
1	(14.5 ounce) can coconut milk
1	tablespoon dark brown sugar
1	tablespoon fish sauce
½	cup pineapple juice
1	cup 1-inch cubes fresh pineapple
1	cup fresh or canned lychee
½	cup red pear tomatoes
1	cup coarsely chopped fresh Thai basil leaves

1. Remove the bones and strip the meat off the duck. Coarsely shred the meat and set aside.

2. In a wok over high heat, heat the oil until very hot. Add the onions and stir-fry for 2 minutes, until the onions begin to wilt. Add the curry paste and stir-fry for 2 minutes.

3. Add ½ of the coconut milk to the wok and blend with the curry paste and onions. Add the sugar and fish sauce, blend well. Add the remaining coconut milk and blend.

4. Add the duck meat. Bring the mixture to a boil, then decrease the heat to medium. Continue to cook and reduce the mixture until it begins to thicken, about 5 minutes. Add the pineapple juice and cook for 2 minutes. Add the pineapple, lychee, and tomatoes and cook for 2 minutes. Turn off the heat and stir in the basil. Serve over jasmine rice.

Serves 6

ingredient notes: *Thai red curry paste is a blend red chiles, coriander roots, garlic, shallots, kaffir lime leaves, lemongrass, shrimp paste, and galangal (Galangal is related to ginger and has a hot, peppery taste). This thick, moist, and spicy blend is traditionally made by pounding the ingredients in a stone mortar and pestle. I use a ready-made paste made by Mae Ploy that has lots of flavor and spice.*

Coconut milk is a liquid made from grated coconut. Canned coconut milk usually has a thick layer of cream at the top, separated from the coconut water below. In this recipe, you want to use the coconut cream, so it's important not to shake the cans of coconut milk before you open them. When you open the can, scoop the thick cream from the top and then add enough liquid to make the 2½ cups.

Thai basil leaves are different from sweet basil: you can identify them by their purple stems and flower heads and dark-green, slightly serrated and pointy leaves. Thai basil has an intense anise flavor and scent.

asian duck stir-fry *with chive crêpes*

This recipe was created out of my love for Chinese roast duck. Being the duck fanatic that I am (besides quail, duck is my favorite poultry), I wanted something that was like Peking duck but with an American twist. I wanted some texture in the filling—the ingredients happened to be what was in the refrigerator at the moment of creation. When you eat these chive crêpes with the sweet and crunchy filling, it drips all over your fingers and then you'll reach for another.

CHIVE CRÊPES

1	cup flour
¼	teaspoon salt
1	cup milk
⅓	cup water
3	eggs
5	tablespoons butter, melted
2	tablespoon chopped fresh chives

DUCK FILLING

1	(4 to 5 pound) Chinese roasted duck, frozen, or preferably freshly cooked from a Chinese vendor
2	cobs fresh corn
½	cup, plus 2 tablespoons oil
Salt	
Freshly ground black pepper	
¼	cup hoisin sauce (Chinese sweet-spicy sauce)
½	cup plum sauce (Chinese duck sauce)
1	medium onion, thinly sliced
½	pound shiitake mushrooms, caps removed and sliced in thirds
2	tablespoons minced fresh ginger
3	cloves garlic, minced
2	cups Chinese cabbage, finely shredded
1	tablespoon chopped fresh chives
¼	cup dried cranberries
½	cup dry-roasted cashews
¼	cup chicken stock

1. To prepare the crêpes, combine the flour and salt in a food processor. Add the milk, water, eggs, and 3 tablespoons of the butter through the feed tube and process until smooth. Transfer to a bowl and mix in the chives.

2. Heat a 6-inch nonstick sauté pan over medium heat. Brush the pan with a little of the remaining 2 tablespoons of butter. Add ¼ cup of the batter to the pan, tilting the pan in a circular motion to spread the batter over the bottom of the pan. Once the batter has set, flip the crêpe to the other side, cook for 10 seconds, and slide it out of the pan onto a serving plate. Continue to cook the crêpes and set aside.

3. To prepare the duck filling, remove the meat and skin from the duck, keeping the meat separate from the skin. Shred the duck meat and place it in a medium mixing bowl. You should have 4 cups of shredded duck meat. Cut the duck skin into thin julienne slices and place on a small plate and set aside.

4. Preheat a grill or grill pan. Rub the corn with a little oil and sprinkle with salt and pepper. On a hot grill or grill pan over high heat, grill the corn for 5 minutes, turning frequently until the corn takes on grill marks. Remove from the heat and cool. With a knife, cut the kernels off the cobs and set aside.

5. In a small sauté pan over medium-high heat, heat ½ cup oil. When the oil is hot, add the duck skin and fry until crisp. Transfer to a paper towel to drain excess oil. Set aside.

6. In a small bowl, mix together the hoisin sauce and the plum sauce.

7. In a large wok or sauté pan over high heat, add the remaining 2 tablespoons of oil. Add the onions and cook until limp. Add the mushrooms, ginger, and garlic and stir-fry for 1 minute. Add the duck meat, corn, Chinese cabbage, chives, cranberries, and cashews. Stir-fry for 2 minutes. Add ½ cup of the plum and hoisin mixture. Stir-fry for 2 minutes. Add

ingredient note: *Plum sauce, also known as duck sauce, is a Chinese condiment made of plums, apricots, and seasonings. It has a sweet-sour flavor and is excellent with duck.*

the chicken stock and stir-fry for another minute. Remove from the heat. Transfer the mixture to a serving bowl. Sprinkle the duck skin over the top.

8. Place the crêpes, duck, and sauce on the table. Each person can assemble their own crêpe: place a heaping tablespoon of the duck mixture in one quadrant of the crepe, fold the crepe over to form a triangle. Serve with the hoisin-plum sauce on the side.

Serves 6

sizzling beef and mushrooms
with sweet garlic over watercress

I love this light stir-fry meal—it's got my favorite beef and bitter greens, a perfect combination. In Hawai'i, watercress is peppery and crunchy and adds to the big flavor of this dish. Frisée, arugula, shredded raw kale, or bok choy can be substituted; they will all wilt when you put the hot stir-fry over them.

4	tablespoons chopped fresh garlic
2	tablespoons fish sauce
2	tablespoons light brown sugar
5	tablespoons peanut oil, for frying
1	pound beef sirloin, cut into 2 by 1/4-inch strips
2	cups thinly sliced red onion
2	tablespoons cider vinegar
2	tablespoons soy sauce
2	tablespoons olive oil
2	teaspoons sugar

Salt

Freshly ground black pepper

6	cups watercress, stems removed
1/2	cup fresh mint, coarsely chopped
1	pound cremini mushrooms, halved

1. To prepare the beef, in a medium bowl, whisk together 2 tablespoons of the garlic, the fish sauce, brown sugar, and 1 1/2 tablespoons of the peanut oil. Add the beef and toss to coat well. Cover and refrigerate for 4 to 6 hours.

2. In a medium bowl, toss together the onions and vinegar. Cover and refrigerate for 1 hour.

3. To make the dressing, in a small bowl, whisk together the soy sauce, olive oil, and sugar. Season with salt, and pepper. Set aside.

4. Remove the beef from the refrigerator 1 hour before cooking. Using a fine-mesh sieve, drain the excess marinade.

5. Just before stir-frying the beef, in a large bowl, toss together the watercress and mint. Remove the onions from the refrigerator, add the dressing, and toss. Place the onions over the watercress and pour the liquid over the watercress.

6. In a large wok over high heat, add 1 tablespoon of the peanut oil and swirl to coat the pan. When the oil is very hot, add the mushrooms and cook for 2 minutes until browned. Transfer to a plate.

7. Add the remaining 2 1/2 tablespoons of the oil to the wok and swirl to coat. Add the beef in one layer and cook for 1 minute. Flip the beef over and sear 1 minute on the other side. Add the remaining 2 tablespoons of garlic and stir-fry the beef for 2 minutes. Add the mushrooms and stir-fry for 1 minute. Pour the beef mixture over the watercress and serve.

Serves 6

chile-cumin-rubbed pork tenderloin
with mango-pineapple salsa

This dish goes back to the days when leftovers became stir-fries on Mondays: a can of pinto beans got combined with leftover roast pork in a tortilla and a jar of salsa became the topper. You could roast this pork for another meal and then use leftovers to make this dish. Either way, it's a simple dish that's perfect for a family meal.

CHILE-CUMIN-RUBBED PORK TENDERLOIN

1	tablespoon chili powder
1½	teaspoons ground cumin
1½	teaspoons garlic powder
1½	teaspoons dried oregano
¼	teaspoon ground cinnamon
1	teaspoon salt
½	teaspoon ground black pepper
1½	pounds pork tenderloin
4	tablespoons oil
¾	cup sliced onions
½	cup fresh corn kernels
1½	cups seeded and diced tomatoes
½	cup cooked black beans
12	(6-inch) flour tortillas
3	tablespoons pumpkin seeds, roasted and salted

MANGO-PINEAPPLE SALSA

½	cup ¼-inch dice fresh mango
½	cup ¼-inch dice fresh pineapple
⅛	cup finely diced red onion
⅛	cup finely diced red bell pepper
1	tablespoon freshly squeezed lime juice
1	tablespoon chopped fresh mint
½	teaspoon sauce from canned chipotle chiles in adobo sauce

Salt

1. To make the rub, in a small bowl, combine the chili powder, cumin, garlic powder, oregano, cinnamon, salt, and pepper.

2. To prepare the pork, cut the tenderloin into 2 by ¼-inch thick strips. Place the pork in a large mixing bowl. Rub the spice mixture all over the pork, tossing well to coat. Cover and refrigerate for 2 hours.

3. Preheat the oven to 350 degrees F.

4. To make the salsa, combine all the ingredients in a bowl and mix thoroughly.

5. Cut 2 sheets of aluminum foil. Wrap 6 tortillas in each sheet of foil. Seal well and place on a baking sheet. Heat in the oven for 15 minutes.

6. To prepare the stir-fry, in a large wok over high heat, add 2 tablespoons of oil and swirl to coat the pan. Add the pork in batches and stir-fry for 2 minutes per batch. Transfer to a plate.

7. Add the remaining 2 tablespoons of oil and swirl to coat the pan. Add the onions and cook for 2 minutes. Add the corn and cook for 2 minutes. Add the pork to the pan and cook for 2 minutes. Add the tomatoes and black beans and cook another 2 to 3 minutes, or until the mixture is hot and cooked through.

8. To serve, place a tortilla on a plate. Spoon the pork mixture onto the tortilla and top with the salsa. Sprinkle with pumpkin seeds.

Serves 6

lamb stir-fry *with eggplant and baby corn*

Lamb isn't often found in stir-fry dishes. I really don't know why because it lends itself well to the technique, and with the right seasonings, the flavor is unbeatable. This is a one-pan, one-dish meal that I know you'll make again and again. Instead of rice, serve it with mashed potatoes.

2	oranges
1	cup chicken stock
4	tablespoons honey
3	tablespoons soy sauce
3	tablespoons oyster sauce
1	tablespoons sambal oelek (Indonesian chile sauce)
1	pound boneless leg of lamb, cut in 1½ by ¼-inch strips

Salt

Freshly ground black pepper

2	tablespoons cornstarch
5	tablespoons oil
1	cup (1-inch) cubes Japanese eggplant
½	pound fresh shiitake mushrooms, stems removed and halved
18	pieces baby corn
2	teaspoons finely minced garlic
1	tablespoon finely minced fresh ginger
1	tablespoon sesame seeds, toasted
½	cup coarsely chopped fresh mint

1. Over a small bowl, zest the oranges using a zester or microplane grater. Peel the oranges and discard the peel. Cut the oranges into sections, allowing the juice to fall into the bowl. Place the orange sections on a plate and set aside.

2. In a small bowl, mix the chicken stock, honey, soy sauce, oyster sauce, sambal oelek, orange zest and juice, blending well. Set aside.

3. On a plate, season the lamb with salt and pepper. Add the cornstarch and mix, coating the lamb well.

4. Heat a wok or large skillet over high heat. Add 3 tablespoons of the oil, swirling the wok to coat it evenly. When the oil is hot but not smoking, add the eggplant and stir-fry until golden and tender, about 2 minutes. Add 1 tablespoon of oil and add the mushrooms; stir-fry until the mushrooms are tender, about 2 minutes. Add the baby corn and stir-fry for 30 seconds. Transfer the mixture to a large bowl.

5. Add the remaining oil to the wok and heat until just smoking. Stir-fry half of the lamb until browned, about 1 minute, and transfer to a bowl. Add the remaining lamb and stir-fry; transfer to the bowl.

6. Add the garlic and ginger to the wok and stir-fry for 15 seconds. Add the chicken stock mixture to the wok and bring to a boil. Continue to boil until the liquid is reduced by one third, about 5 minutes. Return the lamb and vegetables to the wok and stir-fry until well mixed, heated through, and the sauce thickens. Stir in the sesame seeds and mint. Season with salt. Transfer to a serving dish and garnish with the orange sections.

Serves 6

ingredient note: *Japanese or Asian eggplant is a variety that is long and skinny, a little over an inch in diameter. Its skin is usually purple or purple-green and delicate; the flesh is slightly sweet and tender. Look for it in supermarkets or Asian food stores.*

shrimp and scallop stir-fry
with corn and asparagus

Stir-fry dishes don't have to be Asian. It's the technique that matters, not the flavor. This one-dish meal is ideal for a busy family: plan ahead and prepare the ingredients early in the day or the night before; the actual cooking will take just a few minutes. A good egg noodle would be a perfect accompaniment.

4	tablespoons grapeseed oil
1	pound large shrimp, peeled and deveined
1	pound large scallops
½	cup onions, julienned
½	pound oyster mushrooms
¼	cup chopped green onions
1	cup asparagus tips
1	cup fresh corn kernels
2	teaspoons finely minced garlic
1	tablespoon finely minced shallots
1	cup cherry tomatoes
2	tablespoons freshly squeezed lemon juice
1	tablespoon lemon zest
3	tablespoons chiffonade of fresh basil
3	tablespoons extra virgin olive oil

Salt

Freshly ground black pepper

1. In a wok over high heat, add 1 tablespoon of the grapeseed oil, swirling the wok to coat the sides. Add half of the shrimp and stir-fry for 1 minute. Transfer to a plate and repeat with the remaining shrimp.

2. Add 1 tablespoon of the oil and stir-fry half of the scallops for 1 minute. Transfer to a plate and repeat with the remaining scallops.

3. Add the remaining 2 tablespoons of oil to the wok. Add the onions and stir-fry for 2 minutes. Add the mushrooms and green onions and stir-fry for 30 seconds. Add the asparagus tips and corn and stir-fry for 1 minute. Add the garlic and shallots and stir-fry for 30 seconds. Add the shrimp and scallops to the wok mixture. Add the tomatoes and lemon juice and stir-fry for 1 minute. Add the lemon zest, basil, and olive oil and toss together. Remove from the heat and season with salt and pepper. Serve immediately.

Serves 6

lop chong fried rice

The first time I ever tasted lop chong, I ate an entire sausage straight out of the package and then another. I thought it was one of the best things I had ever eaten! You can make fried rice a hundred different ways in Hawai'i, but lop chong adds a unique sweetness and fattiness that I love. When I make fried rice, half of it is rice for texture and the other half is the good stuff for flavor.

4   tablespoons peanut oil, for frying

2   tablespoons peeled and finely diced carrot

⅓   cup diced red onion

3   tablespoons finely minced fresh ginger

¼   cup sliced water chestnuts, quartered

½   cup thinly sliced lop chong (Chinese sausage)

⅓   cup peas, or cooked and shelled edamame (soybeans)

3   cups cooked white rice, cooled

½   teaspoon salt

Pinch of freshly ground black pepper

¼   cup sliced green onions

1. In a large sauté pan, heat the peanut oil over high heat until smoking. Add the carrots and stir-fry for 30 seconds. Add the onion, ginger, water chestnuts, lop chong, and peas one at a time, stir-frying each for 30 seconds before adding the next item. Add the rice, salt, and pepper and continue to stir-fry for 3 minutes, until the rice is heated through. Garnish with the green onions and serve immediately.

Serves 6

ingredient note: *Lop chong is an air-dried Chinese sausage—salty, sweet, and fatty and so delicious! It is made of cured pork, pork fat, beef or duck liver, seasoned with salt, sugar, spices, and rice wine. It is available in supermarkets and Asian food stores. One of the best ways to serve it is to place it on top of steaming rice. Store lop chong in the refrigerator or freezer.*

dry-fried long beans
with cumin and chile

Long beans or yard-long beans are a relative of the black-eyed pea, pencil thin and dark green with a chewy texture. The secret to the taste and texture of long beans is to deep-fry them first, a classic Chinese technique. If you can't find them, use regular green beans. Whichever one you use, you'll find this dish really, really yummy, and it will be hard to stop eating these beans once you start.

1½   **pounds long beans, or fresh green beans**

4   **cups oil**

3   **tablespoons hoisin sauce**

1½   **teaspoons finely minced garlic cloves**

1   **tablespoon sambal oelek (Indonesian chile sauce)**

1   **tablespoon ground cumin**

1   **teaspoon salt**

1. Trim the ends of the beans and cut into 2-inch pieces.

2. In a 2-quart saucepan, heat the oil to 375 degrees F. Line a plate with paper towels. In batches, fry the beans for 1 minute, until the skin just starts to blister. Remove the beans from the oil and drain on the paper towel-lined plate.

3. In a wok over high heat, add 2 teaspoons of the oil from the saucepan. Add the hoisin, garlic, sambal oelek, cumin, and salt and stir together. Add the beans and stir-fry to coat the beans, about 2 minutes. Transfer to a serving plate and serve immediately.

Serves 6

Fish and Seafood

GROWING UP IN DALLAS, I was not an adventuresome eater and I was particularly not a fan of fish. Perhaps it was just the smell of fish: my mom would take me to the fish market and the smell was not pleasant to me at all. Fish always smelled, and it was always mushy.

The worst was when my mother cooked lobster. She got giant lobster tails and cooked them to death. The smell in the house made me ill, and I literally walked through the laundry room and out the door to the playroom next to the garage; I'd hang out there until she was done. Truly, on the days my mother cooked lobster or fish, I tried not to be there. Put a steak in front of me seven days a week and I was a happy camper.

When I came to Hawai'i, it was a whole different story. It was a whole new world of fish that didn't smell fishy when I went to the market or when I went fishing. Once I learned how not to overcook it, fish became a staple in our house.

Today I love fish and love to serve the freshest, tastiest products I can find in my restaurants. There are so many different fish I love. To eat raw, I love 'ahi (yellowfin or bigeye tuna). Raw salmon with a squeeze of lemon and julienned shiso leaf is to die for. I like fattier fish for cooking because they stay moist; fish like monchong and opah are the new mahi mahi for me. I'm also a fan of barramundi from Australia; in fact I'm a big fan of Australian seafood in general.

More than fish, I love shellfish, including lobster, which I used to hate. One of my most decadent meals was in Halifax, Nova Scotia, where I walked into a restaurant and ate as much lobster as I could: two 2-pound lobsters!

Lobster is now at the top of my shellfish list. I like it clean and basic, boiled or steamed with drawn butter on the side. That's the best way to eat lobster. But I love a lobster salad, a lobster stir-fry, lobster with aïoli, and lobster thermidor too.

Mussels are my second favorite shellfish. I had my first bowl of mussels—steamed with herbs, garlic, white wine, and olive oil—in Nice, France. It was a big bowl, served with pommes frites, and when I got down to the last shell, I sopped up the liquid with crusty bread. Mmmmmm.

My mother made me try my first raw oyster. I put it in my mouth, bit into it, and it slid down my throat. I didn't mind the flavor, so I went for a second one. I once ate a good two dozen oysters at Felix's Oyster Bar in New Orleans before throwing in the towel.

Everyone loves shrimp, but I have to admit it's not my favorite. I've been spoiled by fresh shrimp at the shore; today's farm-raised shrimp are just not the same. What makes shrimp really good and flavorful is the sauce; the shrimp provides the texture.

I do love a big bowl of steamed clams with garlic, parsley, and butter swimming in its juices and a big loaf of bread alongside. I love a good clam chowder where every spoonful is just that—full of clams. I can tell no lies: I use fresh and frozen clams in my clam chowder to get the quantity I want in a soup. In my opinion, once you cook clams, you don't know if they're fresh or frozen.

Scallops are my newfound favorite because I've found a source for really fresh scallops. Once you've had them fresh, you can't eat the frozen ones. We now use really fresh, large scallops that are not chemically treated. There's nothing better. But you can't overcook them—I want them translucent in the center.

Getting good fresh crab isn't easy. I love a good Dungeness crab; I love to sit for an hour and a half and pick the meat out. It's the best—better than king crab. Then I like soft-shell crab—panfried in butter with garlic and parsley or blackening spices. Yum.

Fish and shellfish are more than just foods I have to have on my menus. They are delicious foods—light, healthy, and so tasty that I wish I had enjoyed them when I was a kid. But I'm making up for lost time today.

MY FISH COOKING TIPS:

When you're buying a whole fish, it *must* be fresh. It can't be slimy, it can't smell, it can't feel mushy, it can't look dull, its eyes should not be cloudy. It's all about the handling of the fish after it's caught. Remember that a fish could be two or three weeks old, but if it's been handled properly and not sitting out in the air for a week, it will be good. If you live where fish is not always fresh, buy frozen fish that's been handled properly.

When you're frying fish, use a really hot pan. Depending on the thickness of the piece, don't fry it for more than a couple of minutes on each side. If you're baking it, eight to ten minutes will do, not the hour like my mother used to cook it.

Test fish for doneness by poking it: it should give a little, it shouldn't be firm. Don't be afraid to make a slice in the fish to see if it's done. Pull it apart and check it. Take it off the heat or out of the oven when the flesh has barely lost its translucency; by the time it gets to the table the translucency will go away. Fish can be just a little undercooked on the inside when you serve it.

The secret to really crispy fish skin is a light coating of Wondra flour and cooking it in a hot pan with hot oil.

My all-time favorite flavor for fish is simply butter. That said, I do like a sauce with fish and something on top of it—like a beurre blanc sauce with sautéed mushrooms, oven-roasted tomatoes, lemons, olives, fruit salsas, or vegetable salsas. Of course I also like tropical fruit-flavored beurre blancs, or I like to add Asian flavors like wasabi, soy sauce, and miso.

I like to crust fish, hedging my bets a little to keep it moist and succulent. Dip fish in beaten egg whites or, my favorite, a flavored mayonnaise, before crusting it with breadcrumbs, nuts, or other crunchies.

KULA
PUMPKIN

Fish and Seafood

sashimi pizza

I spent years trying to figure out a raw tuna pizza. I did it with rice and fried won ton skins, but finally, with Chef Ivan's help, we came up with a crispy tortilla, the closest thing to a pizza crust. I wanted raw tuna with a sauce; I wanted Asian flavors. The edamame hummus adds texture. It's an Italian-Asian pizza!

EDAMAME HUMMUS

2   cups cooked and shelled edamame
     (soybeans)

8   cloves garlic

1/2 cup oil

Salt

SOY-SESAME AÏOLI

2   teaspoons Colman's dry mustard

2   teaspoons water

1   small onion, cut into chunks

2   tablespoons soy sauce

2   tablespoons sesame oil

1/4 cup oil

2   teaspoons dashi (Japanese soup stock)

1   tablespoon sugar

1   teaspoon freshly ground black pepper

2   teaspoons salt

1   cup mayonnaise

CRISPY-FRIED ONIONS

1   cup flour

Salt

Freshly ground black pepper

1   onion, sliced very thin

Peanut oil, for frying

1. To prepare the hummus, purée all the ingredients in a food processor until smooth.

2. To prepare the aïoli, mix the dry mustard and water to form a thick paste. Transfer the mustard to a blender and add all the other ingredients except the mayonnaise. Blend well, then add the mayonnaise and blend again.

3. To fry the onions, mix together the flour, salt, and pepper. Coat the onion slices in the flour. Heat about 1 inch of oil in a saucepan to 375 degrees F. Fry the onion slices in small batches until crisp and golden brown. Remove from the oil and drain on paper towels.

TORTILLA "CRUST"

6   (6-inch) flour tortillas

¼   cup kabayaki sauce (Japanese soy-based sauce)

1   pound sashimi-grade 'ahi, thinly sliced

¼   cup finely shredded red cabbage

¼   cup kaiware sprouts (Japanese radish sprouts)

2   tablespoons tobiko caviar (flying fish roe)

4. To assemble the pizzas, preheat the oven to 400 degrees F. Brush each flour tortilla with kabayaki sauce and place on a baking sheet. Bake in the oven until crispy, about 5 to 8 minutes. Remove from the oven.

5. Spread each tortilla with the hummus. Top with the 'ahi and cabbage. Sprinkle with crispy onions. Drizzle with aïoli, sprinkle with sprouts, and finish with a topping of tobiko.

Makes 6 pizzas

ingredient notes: *Dashi is a Japanese soup stock based on seaweed and dried fish. It can be made from scratch, but instant dashi powders and cubes are available in Asian grocery stores.*

Kabayaki sauce is a soy-based sauce made from eel bones, soy sauce, mirin, sugar, and puréed apples. It's sweet and salty, and it's available in Japanese food markets.

Kaiware sprouts are Japanese radish sprouts with light green stems, a small leafy top, and a spicy kick.

cajun spice-blackened 'ahi
with shiitake mushrooms

Tom Newcomer, my chef at Joe's in Wailea, brought this recipe to the restaurant, a dish he created at another restaurant. People followed him to Joe's when they heard it was on the menu, and now the dish finds itself on the menu at various times. Tom always has the ingredients around so he can make it on a moment's notice for the diner addicted to the Sesame Vinaigrette and the Cilantro-Ginger Oil.

CILANTRO-GINGER OIL

1/2	cup olive oil
3	tablespoons chopped fresh cilantro
2	tablespoons finely chopped fresh ginger
2	cloves garlic, minced

SESAME VINAIGRETTE

3	tablespoons sesame oil
4	tablespoons tahini (sesame paste)
1/4	cup soy sauce
1/4	cup water
1/8	cup freshly squeezed orange juice
2	tablespoons Dijon-style mustard
2	tablespoons sugar
1/8	cup rice wine vinegar

1. To prepare the Cilantro-Ginger Oil, in a small saucepan over medium heat, add the olive oil. Heat until warm then add the cilantro, ginger, and garlic. Heat for 2 minutes. Remove from the heat and set aside to cool. Cover and let steep for 24 hours. Strain the oil through a fine-mesh strainer into an airtight container. Cover and refrigerate until ready to use.

2. To make the vinaigrette, in a blender on low speed, add all the ingredients. Blend until thoroughly incorporated.

3. To prepare the mushrooms, in a large sauté pan over high heat, add 2 tablespoons of the oil. When the oil is hot, add the mushrooms and sauté until lightly browned. Sprinkle with 1 teaspoon of the spice mix. Remove from the heat and set aside on the stovetop.

ingredient notes: *'Ahi is Hawai'i's prized fish—yellowfin or bigeye tunas caught in deep Pacific waters. We love it raw as sashimi in the islands, seared on the edges, or cut into bite-sized morsels and seasoned in a famous local dish known as poke. Fresh 'ahi is found everywhere in Hawai'i; look for Hawaiian 'ahi in mainland cities too.*

Sashimi-grade 'ahi is the best you can buy, the top grade. When it's in its prime, fresh 'ahi should have a deep red color, firm texture, and a glistening surface that indicates high fat content. Be wary of 'ahi that is bright red as it may have been treated with carbon monoxide to preserve its color and fresh looks. Always buy fresh fish from a reputable fishmonger.

Tahini is sesame seed paste, found in Middle Eastern food stores or health food stores.

FISH

4	tablespoons oil
1	pound fresh shiitake mushrooms, cleaned, stems removed, and sliced
½	cup Blackening Spice Mix (page 13)
2	pounds sashimi-grade 'ahi, cut into 8 steaks
¼	cup green onions, cut diagonally, for garnish

4. To prepare the 'ahi, place the remaining spice mix in a shallow plate. Coat the 'ahi well with the spices. In a cast iron skillet over high heat, add the remaining 2 tablespoons of the oil. Sear the 'ahi very quickly on all sides. The spices will turn black. Do not overcook the fish—it should be very rare in the center and seared on all the edges. Transfer the fish to a cutting board. Slice the 'ahi into ½-inch slices.

5. To serve, place the mushrooms on a platter. Pour the sesame vinaigrette around and over mushrooms. Place the 'ahi slices over the mushrooms. Drizzle the fish with Cilantro-Ginger Oil. Garnish with green onions.

Serves 8

smoked salmon pinwheels
with chipotle-chile fresh fruit salsa

Ever since I was a kid, I've loved the flavor of smoked salmon, and I'd always be the first to pick it off the Sunday brunch platters at home. When I started catering, I wanted to use smoked salmon, but it had to be pretty and something you could pick up with your fingers. Using a tortilla to hold it and roll it works really well, and when you slice it on the diagonal, you get a pretty bite of food. Don't limit yourself to smoked salmon for this recipe: crab, chopped lobster, or grilled chicken can work well too.

SALMON PINWHEELS

4   ounces goat cheese, at room temperature

4   ounces cream cheese, at room temperature

2   tablespoons heavy cream

6   (10-inch) flour tortillas

12 ounces thinly sliced cold-smoked salmon

1/4 cup finely chopped green onions

1/4 cup finely chopped fresh cilantro

1/4 cup finely chopped fresh chives

FRESH FRUIT SALSA

3   cups (1/4-inch) diced fruit (such as pineapple, kiwi, papaya, strawberries, mango, or other seasonal choice)

1/2 cup finely chopped red onion

Zest of 1 lime

2 to 4 teaspoons liquid from canned chipotle chiles

2   tablespoons chopped fresh mint

2   tablespoons chopped fresh cilantro

1. To prepare the pinwheels, in a small bowl, combine the goat cheese, cream cheese, and cream; blend until smooth. Spread the cheese mixture onto the tortillas, covering to the edges of the tortilla. Lay the salmon slices over the cheese. Sprinkle with the green onions, cilantro, and chives. Roll each tortilla up tightly and wrap in plastic wrap. Refrigerate until ready to serve.

2. To make the fruit salsa, place all ingredients in a bowl and gently toss.

3. To serve, cut each tortilla roll into slices on the diagonal about 3/4-inch thick. Serve with salsa alongside.

Serves 6

ingredient note: *Chipotle chiles are dried, smoked jalapeños, usually found pickled or canned in adobo sauce. The latter is what I keep in my pantry to add a smoky and spicy note to this dish.*

dynamite salmon *with coconut-curry baby bok choy and jasmine rice*

When looking for a way to spice up salmon, we turned for inspiration to "dynamite scallops," a popular sushi bar preparation in which mayonnaise and fiery chile sauce embellish fish. The delicious result was—well, dynamite! We always use wild salmon—it's more flavorful and better for you. When you serve the bok choy, serve it in a covered dish. When the lid is removed, the aroma will make everyone happy before they take a single bite.

SALMON

6	(6-ounce) fresh salmon fillets
1¹/₂	cups mayonnaise
¹/₄	cup chopped green onion
2	tablespoons tobiko caviar (flying fish roe)
1	tablespoon white miso (soybean paste)
1	teaspoon dashi (Japanese soup stock)
1	tablespoon sambal oelek (Indonesian chile sauce)

JASMINE RICE

2	cups jasmine rice
3	cups water
3	stalks lemongrass, cut into 2-inch pieces and crushed
1	teaspoon salt
4	teaspoons furikake (Japanese seaweed mix)

COCONUT-CURRY BABY BOK CHOY

1	(14-ounce) can coconut milk
4	teaspoons Thai green curry paste
1	teaspoon fish sauce
Juice of one lime	
8	heads baby bok choy, halved lengthwise

1. Preheat the oven to 400 degrees F.

2. To prepare the salmon, grease a baking sheet with vegetable spray and place the salmon fillets 1 inch apart on the sheet.

3. In a small bowl, mix the mayonnaise, green onion, tobiko, miso, dashi, and sambal oelek with a whisk until all the ingredients are well blended. Spoon the sauce evenly over the salmon fillets, covering each fillet completely. You can refrigerate the salmon at this point while preparing the rice and bok choy.

4. To make the rice, in a 2-quart saucepan over medium-high heat, add the rice, water, lemongrass, and salt and bring to a boil. Decrease the heat to a simmer, cover, and cook until the water is completely absorbed, about 20 minutes. Remove from the heat and let stand for 10 minutes. Remove the lemongrass and fluff the rice with a fork. Keep warm.

5. To prepare the bok choy, in a small saucepan over low heat, heat the coconut milk with the curry paste, fish sauce, and lime juice. Bring to a simmer. Add the bok choy, cover and simmer until cooked through, about 5 minutes. Season to taste with more fish sauce. Keep warm.

6. Remove the salmon from the refrigerator. Bake the salmon in the oven for 10 to 15 minutes, or until the salmon is cooked and the dynamite sauce is golden brown.

7. To serve, place the salmon on a plate with the bok choy and the jasmine rice alongside. Sprinkle the rice with the furikake.

Serves 6

ingredient notes: *Furikake is a condiment of seaweed bits, sesame seeds, fish, and salt that is usually sprinkled over rice. It is also used to coat fish, poultry, and meats and to enhance the flavor of many foods.*

Baby bok choy is a Chinese green vegetable with green leaf tips and a white stalk. Several leaves make up the head that is usually 6 inches in length. Baby bok choy can be steamed, stir-fried, or braised.

Tobiko is a kind of caviar known as flying fish roe, usually orange in color but it could be green, indicating it is wasabi flavored. Look for tobiko in Asian food stores or fish markets.

pumpkin seed-crusted fresh catch
with chipotle-honey sauce

There's nothing better than toasted pumpkin seeds—except a toasted pumpkin-seed crust for fish. Crusting fish is one of my trademarks: it keeps fish moist and gives me a little leeway if the fish gets overcooked, especially on an airliner. Crusting also adds flavor without taking away from the taste of the fish itself. This dish, with its American-Southwestern flair, was created for Joe's in Wailea. Mashed potatoes would be a perfect accompaniment alongside the Lemon Beurre Blanc sauce.

FISH

1/2   cup mayonnaise

1   tablespoon cumin seed, roasted and ground

1   teaspoon salt

2   teaspoons dried oregano

1/4   cup panko (Japanese breadcrumbs)

1/2   cup pumpkin seeds, roasted and salted

8   (6-ounce) fillets fresh mahi mahi, or other fresh white fish

     Salt and freshly ground black pepper

2   tablespoons oil

CHIPOTLE-HONEY SAUCE

1/4   cup puréed chipotle chile peppers in sauce

1/4   cup honey

3   tablespoons freshly squeezed lemon juice

1   tablespoon Demi-Glace (page 12), or vegetable stock

LEMON BEURRE BLANC SAUCE

1   cup, plus 2 teaspoons butter, cut into small cubes, chilled

1   tablespoon chopped shallots

1   cup white wine

1 1/2 cups heavy cream

1. In a small bowl with a wire whisk, mix together the mayonnaise, cumin, salt, and oregano. Set aside.

2. Place the panko and pumpkin seeds in a food processor. Pulse 10 to 12 times to coarsely chop together. Transfer to a shallow dish and set aside.

3. To make the Chipotle-Honey Sauce, combine the chipotle purée, honey, lemon juice, and demi-glace in a small saucepan over medium heat. Heat for 5 minutes. Remove from the heat and keep warm.

4. To prepare the beurre blanc sauce, in a saucepan over medium heat, melt the 2 teaspoons of butter. Add the shallots and cook for 2 minutes. Add the white wine, bring to a boil, decrease the heat and continue to cook, reducing the liquid until there is 1 tablespoon left. Add the cream and reduce by half or until slightly thickened. Add the lemon juice and blend well. Strain the sauce through a fine-mesh sieve into another saucepan. Over low heat with a wire whisk, add the remaining 1 cup of butter, a few pieces at a time. Make sure the sauce does not boil; the sauce will become shiny and thick. Season with salt and white pepper. Remove from the heat and keep warm.

5. To prepare the fish, season both sides of the fish with salt and pepper. Spread 1 tablespoon of the mayonnaise mixture on one side of fish. Coat that side with the pumpkin seed crust, pressing firmly so that the coating sticks. Repeat with all of the fish fillets.

6. In a large sauté pan over medium heat, add the oil. Place the fish crust side down and cook for two minutes or until the crust is golden brown. Turn the fish over, reduce the heat to low and cook the fish another 3 minutes, or until the fish is just cooked through.

1   tablespoon freshly squeezed lemon
     juice

Salt

Freshly ground white pepper

7. To serve, place the fish on individual plates. Drizzle with 3 tablespoons of the beurre blanc and 3 tablespoons of the Chipotle-Honey Sauce.

Serves 8

ingredient note: *To toast the pumpkin seeds, place them in an ungreased, small frying pan over medium heat. Toast for several minutes, shaking the pan, until lightly browned. You can also toast them on a baking sheet in a 300-degree-F oven. Shake the pan every few minutes so that the seeds toast evenly.*

snapper *with saffron-crab cream sauce, asparagus, and purple sweet potatoes*

My cooks come up with two fish specials every night at Hali'imaile General Store and Joe's in Wailea, allowing them to get creative in the kitchen. Ross, one of the cooks at Joe's, came up with this special one night. There are nights that people love the special and there are nights that people LOVE it. People couldn't stop talking about this one.

SWEET POTATOES

2	pounds Moloka'i purple sweet potatoes, peeled and cut into 2-inch cubes
1/4	cup milk, at room temperature
2	tablespoons butter, at room temperature

Salt

Freshly ground black pepper

ASPARAGUS

1	tablespoon freshly squeezed lemon juice

Salt

24	pieces jumbo asparagus

SAFFRON-CRAB CREAM SAUCE

2	teaspoons butter
1	tablespoon minced shallots
1/2	cup white wine
2	cups rich fish stock (page 11)
1/2	teaspoon saffron threads
1 1/2	cups heavy cream
1	cup blue crabmeat

1. To prepare the potatoes, place the potatoes in a pot of salted water and bring to a boil over high heat. Decrease the heat to low and cook the potatoes until tender, about 20 minutes. Drain the potatoes in a colander.

2. Place the milk and the butter in a bowl. Using a potato ricer, rice the potatoes into the bowl. With a rubber spatula, mix the potatoes thoroughly with the butter and milk. Season with salt and pepper. Set aside and keep warm.

3. To prepare the asparagus, bring water to a boil in a large sauté pan. Have ready a bowl of ice water. Decrease the heat so the water simmers. Add some salt to the water along with the lemon juice. Add the asparagus and cook for about 3 minutes or until just tender, drain, and transfer to the bowl of ice water. When the asparagus is cool, drain, and place in an ovenproof dish. Keep warm.

4. To make the sauce, in a saucepan over medium-high heat, melt the butter. Add the shallots and cook for 1 minute. Add the white wine, bring to a boil, decrease the heat and continue to cook until the wine has reduced to 1 tablespoon. Add the fish stock and the saffron, and reduce the liquid by one-half. Add the cream and reduce by one-half, or until the sauce is thick. Strain the sauce through a fine-mesh strainer into another saucepan. Add the crabmeat to the sauce. Stir, set aside, and keep warm. (A great way to keep sauces warm and intact for up to 2 to 3 hours, especially cream sauces and beurre blancs, is to store them in a small thermos you keep just for sauces.)

continued on page 76

FISH

8   (6-ounce) snapper fillets

Salt

Freshly ground black pepper

¼   cup Wondra flour

2   tablespoons butter

2   tablespoons olive oil

8   fresh thyme sprigs, for garnish

5. To prepare the fish, season the fish fillets with salt and pepper. Place the Wondra in a shallow dish and coat the fish lightly with the flour. In a large sauté pan over high heat, melt the butter and olive oil together. Place the fish into the sauté pan, in batches, and cook on each side for about 2 minutes. When the fish is cooked, transfer it to a warm plate.

6. To serve, place ⅓ cup of the sweet potatoes in the center of 8 plates. Divide the asparagus among the plates and place the spears on top of the potatoes. Place the fish on top of the asparagus. Ladle about ¼ cup of the sauce over the fish. Garnish each plate with a fresh thyme sprig.

Serves 8

ingredient notes: *Moloka'i purple sweet potatoes are a delicious variety of sweet potatoes found on Moloka'i and on other islands in Hawai'i. I love their vibrant purple color! If you can't find this variety, yellow varieties will do.*

Saffron is probably the most expensive spice in the world. Thank goodness you only need a little for saffron to work its magic, adding its distinctive pungent aroma and deep yellow color to food. Before using the threads, chop them and crush them to release their essence.

curry-crab wontons
with mango-chutney plum sauce

I frequently prepare multicourse feasts when visiting friends on the mainland. One of these dinners was a six-course meal in New York City. As I was shopping, I spotted some lump crabmeat, fresh and already picked over. Crab wontons, I thought, and I came up with this recipe. Eight people ate forty wontons as soon as they came out of the fryer, then proceeded to eat their six-course meal! This is one of those recipes you hate to give out: you want people to think there's a hundred ingredients in it, but, really, it's so simple!

MANGO-CHUTNEY PLUM SAUCE

1/2   **cup mango chutney**

1/2   **cup plum sauce (Chinese duck sauce)**

1/4   **cup plain yogurt**

CURRY-CRAB FILLING

1   **pound lump crabmeat**

1   **pound cream cheese, at room temperature**

1   **tablespoon chopped fresh cilantro**

1   **tablespoon thinly sliced green onions**

2   **teaspoons oil**

2   **tablespoons yellow Madras curry powder**

Salt

1   **package wonton wrappers**

Peanut oil, for frying

> **ingredient note:** *Madras curry powder is a blend of many spices, herbs, and seeds used to make Indian curries. Madras is the former name of the city in southern India that is now called Chennai; it refers to a spicier blend of commercially available curry powders.*

1. To make the sauce, place the chutney in a food processor and pulse until smooth. Add the plum sauce and yogurt and process until mixed well. Transfer to a serving bowl. Set aside.

2. To prepare the crab filling, place the crab in a bowl and pick over it to make sure there are no pieces of shell or cartilage.

3. In a medium bowl, blend the cream cheese with the cilantro and the green onions.

4. In a small nonstick sauté pan over medium-high heat, add the 2 teaspoons of oil. Add the curry powder and cook until fragrant. Remove from the heat and transfer the curry powder to the cream cheese mixture; stir to incorporate. Add the crab to the cream cheese mixture and without overmixing, incorporate the crab into the cream cheese mixture. Season with salt.

5. To make the wontons, moisten the edges of a wrapper with water. Place a generous teaspoon of filling in the center of the wrapper, fold the wrapper in half to form a triangle and seal the edges together. Place the wonton on a plate or baking pan. Continue to wrap the wontons until all the filling is used.

6. In a large saucepan over high heat, heat the oil to 375 degrees F. Drop 3 to 4 wontons into the hot oil, and cook until golden brown, turning once. Transfer the wontons to a plate lined with paper towels to drain. Continue to fry the wontons, making sure the oil returns to 375 degrees F between batches. Serve immediately with the sauce.

Serves 6

shrimp scorpio

What's old is new again. This is a recipe from the very early days of Hali'imaile General Store; today we serve it at Joe's in Wailea on top of angel hair pasta. It's a dish that's simple to prepare for a family meal, offering a zesty balance of sweet, salty, and spicy flavors accented by the hit of sambuca.

6   tablespoons olive oil

1   cup finely chopped onion

6   cloves garlic, finely chopped

$1/2$ teaspoon red pepper flakes

3   cups seeded and coarsely chopped Roma tomatoes

2   tablespoons capers

$1/2$ cup pitted kalamata olives

6   tablespoons sambuca (anise-flavored liqueur)

Salt

Freshly ground black pepper

3   tablespoons fresh chopped dill

2   tablespoons finely chopped fresh parsley

1   pound angel hair pasta

24   large shrimp, peeled and deveined

$1/2$ cup crumbled feta cheese

ingredient note: *Sambuca is a clear Italian anise-flavored liqueur based on the elderberry. It is often served with a few floating coffee beans.*

1. In a large sauté pan over medium-high heat, add 3 tablespoons of the olive oil. When the oil is hot, add the onions and cook for 3 minutes. Add the garlic, red pepper flakes, and tomatoes and cook for 2 minutes more. Add the capers and the olives and cook for 1 minute.

2. Move the tomato mixture to one side of the sauté pan. Add 3 tablespoons of the sambuca to the opposite side of the pan. Light a match to the sambuca to burn off the alcohol. When the flame has subsided, mix the sambuca into the tomato mixture. Season with salt and pepper. Add the dill and the parsley and toss together. Remove the pan from the heat and set aside.

3. Bring a large pot of salted water to a boil. Add the pasta and cook to al dente, about 8 minutes.

4. While the pasta is cooking, in another sauté pan over high heat, add 2 tablespoons of the olive oil. When the oil is hot, add half the shrimp and sauté for 3 minutes, or until just cooked. Transfer the shrimp to the pan with the tomato sauce. Add the remaining oil as necessary and sauté the remaining shrimp.

5. After cooking all the shrimp, add the remaining 3 tablespoons of sambuca to the pan and deglaze the pan, scraping any bits off the bottom of the pan. Add the deglazed liquid to the shrimp and tomato mixture and stir to incorporate well. Keep warm.

6. Drain the pasta in a colander and pour the pasta into a large serving bowl. Pour the sauce over the pasta. Top the sauce with the feta cheese and serve.

Serves 6

asian fried calamari

Who has the best fried calamari? Of course, I'd have to say Joe's in Wailea where this version has been on the menu since day one. It's the batter that has all the flavor; the calamari is there for its tender texture. These golden-brown fried morsels are just the best!

CHILE DIPPING SAUCE

2	cups Thai sweet chile sauce
2	tablespoons freshly squeezed lime juice
2	teaspoons fish sauce
1	tablespoon minced shallots
1/4	cup water

CALAMARI

2	pounds calamari, cleaned (see ingredient notes below)
2	cups milk
2	cups flour
4	tablespoons chili powder
4	tablespoons sweet paprika
4	tablespoons dried dill
2	tablespoons ginger powder
2	tablespoons garlic powder

Salt

Freshly ground black pepper

Oil for frying

1. To make the dipping sauce, whisk together all the ingredients in a bowl. Transfer to a serving bowl and set aside.

2. To prepare the calamari, line a baking dish with paper towels. Cut the calamari tentacles off the body and cut the body into $1/2$-inch circles. Place the calamari pieces in the baking dish. Dry the calamari with the paper towels; discard the paper towels. Pour the milk over the calamari and set aside.

3. In a large bowl, mix together the flour, chili powder, paprika, dill, ginger, garlic, salt, and pepper.

4. Line a plate with paper towels. In a large saucepan or deep fryer, heat 3 to 4 inches of oil to 375 degrees F. Using a colander, drain the calamari. In batches, dredge the calamari in the seasoned flour. Shake off any excess flour and fry the calamari in the oil until golden brown. Transfer the fried calamari to the plate to drain the excess oil. Transfer to a serving plate, and serve with the dipping sauce.

Serves 8

ingredient notes: *Thai sweet chile sauce is a sweet, tangy, spicy sauce, just one of the best all around condiments for grilled or fried chicken and seafood of all kinds. It can be found in Southeast Asian food stores.*

Calamari is best purchased already cleaned and ready to use, usually in the freezer case of your supermarket. But if it does require cleaning, here's what to do: Grasp the head and gently pull it from the body, cleaning any remaining innards with the dull edge of a knife. Pull out the translucent quill. Peel the purplish skin off the body with your fingers. Cut the tentacles off above the beak, just above the eyes. Squeeze the tentacles and remove the beak. Rinse the tentacles and body, and dry well. Slice the body into rings; tentacles can be divided into bite-sized portions, depending on the size.

rock shrimp tempura
with three dipping sauces

This recipe came about because I wanted to use Chinese take-out containers to present a dish. In other words, looks decided the dish. We serve these crispy morsels with the popcorn pouring out of a take-out container and the dipping sauces alongside. Not a bit is ever left uneaten.

SOY-SESAME AÏOLI (PAGE 64)

SPICY MISO SAUCE

2	tablespoons Colman's dry mustard
2	tablespoons water
¹/₂	cup red miso (Japanese soybean paste)
¹/₂	cup mirin (Japanese sweet cooking wine)
2	tablespoons sugar

TRUFFLE-HONEY SAUCE

1	cup honey
1	tablespoon truffle oil
1	teaspoon finely ground black pepper
¹/₄	cup water

SHRIMP

¹/₂	cup all-purpose flour
¹/₂	cup cornstarch
1	teaspoon baking soda
1	teaspoon baking powder
¹/₂	teaspoon salt
1	egg
²/₃	cup cold milk
6	cups canola oil
1¹/₂	pounds rock shrimp
1	cup mixed baby greens (such as arugula, oakleaf, mizuna, tatsoi, red and green lettuce)
2	cups popped popcorn

1. To prepare the miso sauce, in a small bowl using a wire whisk, mix the mustard with the water until it forms a smooth paste. Add the miso and whisk to blend. Slowly add half of the mirin. Add the sugar and whisk thoroughly. Add the rest of the mirin and mix well. Transfer to serving bowl and set aside.

2. To make the truffle sauce, in a small bowl using a wire whisk, mix together all the ingredients. Transfer to serving bowl and set aside.

3. To make the tempura batter, in a small bowl, sift together the flour, cornstarch, baking soda, baking powder, and salt. In a medium bowl using a wire whisk, beat the egg for 30 seconds. Slowly whisk the milk into the beaten egg. Add the dry ingredients and stir until just mixed. The mixture will still have lumps, but do not overmix. Refrigerate the batter until ready to use.

4. Place the oil in a large saucepan over high heat. Heat the oil to 375 degrees F.

5. To prepare the shrimp, pat the rock shrimp dry with paper towels and place on a plate. Remove the batter from the refrigerator. With a whisk, lightly stir the batter.

6. Line a platter with paper towels. Add the shrimp to the batter in batches. Transfer the battered shrimp to a strainer. Place the strainer on a plate to catch the batter drippings. Using tongs, place the shrimp into the hot oil. Fry until the shrimp turns golden brown. When the shrimp are cooked, transfer them to the platter to drain. Repeat until all the shrimp are fried, making sure the oil returns to 375 degrees F between each batch.

continued on page 82

ingredient notes: *Red miso is a Japanese soybean paste made of soybeans and rice. It is more robust in flavor and saltier than white miso.*

Mirin is a syrupy liquid made from fermented glutinous rice and distilled grain alcohol. True mirin is naturally brewed and has about 12 percent alcoholic content. In cooking, the alcohol is burned off and the sweet flavor remains.

7. To serve, place the greens on a plate. Sprinkle the popcorn over the greens. Heap on the shrimp. Serve with sauces in bowls on the side.

Serves 6

pan-seared scallops *with butternut squash purée and lemon beurre blanc*

I often sell myself to benefit various charities. As an auction item, I offer to prepare an extravagant dinner party, a multicourse feast at my home. When auctioned off, this usually brings in thousands of dollars for the charity. When I do one of these dinners, I like to get creative and come up with interesting, different dishes. This is one of the dishes I came up with for a charity dinner; it has now become a menu item at Hali'imaile General Store—except we don't put a dollop of sevruga caviar on top of the scallop like I did for the original dinner.

SQUASH PURÉE

4	cups peeled and cubed butternut squash
2	tablespoons butter
1/4	cup heavy cream at room temperature
1	teaspoon nutmeg

Salt

Freshly ground white pepper

1. To make the squash purée, in a saucepan filled with water over high heat, add the butternut squash. Bring to a boil, cover, decrease the heat to medium, and cook for 10 minutes, or until the squash is fork tender. When the squash is cooked, drain it in a colander and transfer the squash to a bowl. Using an immersion blender, purée the squash. Add the butter, cream, and nutmeg. Season with salt and pepper. Purée again until all the ingredients are blended together. Set aside and keep warm.

2. To prepare the sauce, melt 2 teaspoons of butter in a saucepan over medium heat. Add the shallots and cook for 2 minutes. Add the white wine, bring to a boil, decrease the heat, and continue to cook until the

LEMON BEURRE BLANC SAUCE

1   cup, plus 2 teaspoons butter, cut into 1/2-inch cubes

1   tablespoon shallots

1/2   cup white wine

1   cup heavy cream

1   tablespoon freshly squeezed lemon juice

2   teaspoons lemon zest

Salt

Freshly ground white pepper

18   large scallops

1   tablespoon oil 1 tablespoon butter

2   tablespoons Chive Oil (page 14)

liquid is reduced to 1 tablespoon. Add the cream and cook until the cream is thick and reduced by one-half.

3. Using a fine-mesh strainer, strain the cream into another saucepan. Place the saucepan over low heat. Add the lemon juice and whisk into the cream. Add the remaining 1 cup of butter, a few pieces at a time, and whisk into the cream. Keep adding the butter until the sauce becomes silky and slightly thick, whisking constantly so that the sauce does not break. Add the lemon zest. Season with salt and pepper. Remove the sauce from the heat and keep warm, whisking frequently.

4. To prepare the scallops, season the scallops with salt and pepper. In a sauté pan over medium-high heat, add the oil and butter. Cook the scallops, in batches, for 3 minutes on each side. When they are cooked, transfer them to a plate and keep warm.

5. To serve, place three pools of butternut squash purée on a plate. Place three scallops on top of the purée. Drizzle the sauce over the scallops. Drizzle the Chive Oil around the plate.

Serves 6

ingredient notes: *Look for dry, diver, or day boat scallops. "Dry" refers to scallops that have not been treated with chemicals and soaked in water; the chemicals cause them to retain water so they have a longer shelf life. "Diver" and "dayboat" mean the sea scallops have been harvested by divers and taken to shore the same day. Fresh, untreated scallops are the best—moist and tender as scallops should be.*

Shallots—those small, golden-brown onion-like orbs—pack a lot of subtle onion-garlic flavor. That's why I like to use them, especially when I'm making butter sauces where they give some depth of flavor without overpowering delicate flavors. Caramelized shallots, like caramelized onions, are just simply wonderful. And shallots in a salad dressing are a must!

Casseroles

CASSEROLES IN OUR HOUSE were an afterthought, a mishmash of leftovers with a white sauce or canned cream of mushroom soup. My mom did make a chicken enchilada casserole sometimes, layered instead of rolled. When she did a tuna-noodle casserole, she used canned Chicken of the Sea albacore tuna, canned La Sueur peas, sliced mushrooms out of a jar, canned cream of celery or cream of mushroom soup, and kosher squiggly noodles with crushed potato chips on top. There also was her version of chicken divan: frozen broccoli, chicken, and canned cheddar cheese soup. Or, when we were celebrating, we'd put on our short white gloves and go to Neiman's for turkey mornay: turkey slices, broccoli, and mornay sauce, browned under the broiler.

Many of us remember these dishes from our childhood, concocted when canned soups became the replacement for sauces made from scratch. It is the sauce, after all, that binds together all the elements of a casserole, mainly protein and starch. Casserole ingredients, usually cooked, are enrobed in the sauce and topped off with something that becomes crunchy when it bakes.

But I remember when I fell in love with a casserole: I was at a friend's house when I was twelve or thirteen years old, and her mom made a chicken fettuccine casserole. It was so good I went into the kitchen and asked her mom to write down the recipe for me!

Casseroles are so easy; you can make one ahead, make an extra one to freeze, and use up those leftovers! These are some of my favorites.

Casseroles

chicken fettuccine casserole

My mother always roasted whole chickens in the oven or put them on the rotisserie. And she always made extras because you can do so much with the leftovers—like shredding up a chicken to make this casserole, my version of a casserole I used to eat at my best friend's house. It's a flavorful combination of ingredients, bound together with a creamy, luscious sauce enhanced with sherry. It's one of my all-time favorite casseroles, full of old-fashioned familiar taste, and it's the perfect one-dish meal.

12	ounces egg fettuccine
1/4	cup, plus 4 teaspoons butter
1/2	cup chopped onion
2	cups sliced fresh shiitake mushrooms
Salt	
Freshly ground black pepper	
1/4	cup flour
1	cup milk
1	cup chicken stock
2	teaspoons salt
1 1/4	cups sour cream
1/3	cup sherry
1	large chicken, cooked, boned, and shredded
1/2	cup sliced black olives
1/3	cup sliced and halved water chestnuts
1	cup cooked spinach leaves (about 1 pound fresh)
1	tablespoon dried tarragon
1	cup grated Monterey Jack cheese
1/2	cup grated Parmigiano-Reggiano cheese

1. Preheat the oven to 325 degrees F. Grease a 3-quart ovenproof casserole dish.

2. Bring a large pot of salted water to a boil. Add the fettuccine and cook about 8 to 10 minutes, or until just al dente. Drain and place the fettuccine in a large bowl.

3. In a small sauté pan, melt 1 teaspoon of the butter over medium high-heat. Add the onion and cook until translucent. Remove from the pan and set aside.

4. In the same sauté pan, melt 3 teaspoons of the butter. Add the mushrooms and cook over medium-high heat until lightly browned. Season with salt and pepper. Remove from the heat.

5. To make the sauce, place a saucepan over medium-high heat and melt the remaining 1/4 cup butter. When the butter has melted, whisk in the flour and cook, stirring, for about 2 minutes. Remove the pan from the heat and slowly add the milk and the chicken stock, whisking continuously. Place the pan back on the heat and continue to cook until the sauce has thickened. Stir in 2 teaspoons of salt, the sour cream, and sherry, blending well. Remove from the heat.

6. Add one cup of the sauce to the fettuccine and toss together. Add the onion, mushrooms, chicken, olives, water chestnuts, spinach, and tarragon, and mix together. Add the remaining sauce, and season with salt and pepper. Transfer the mixture to the casserole and top with the grated cheeses. Bake for 25 to 30 minutes until bubbly and browned on the top.

Serves 6

ingredient note: *Parmigiano-Reggiano is Parmesan cheese, the authentic one from Italy, aged for almost two years before it is sold. I prefer to use this because of its good flavor and the way it melts and incorporates into sauces. It costs a little more, but it's far better than the stuff in the green box. It's available at supermarkets and in cheese shops everywhere, but if you can't find it, at least try to use a good-quality Parmesan cheese.*

chicken, sausage, and shiitake mushroom pot pie

I cannot tell a lie: Swanson chicken pot pies were big in our house when I was growing up. When I ate my pie, I ate the crust and the chicken pieces out of it; I didn't like all the other stuff. But when I started cooking, I learned that you could make your own chicken pot pie and it could be really good.

This recipe is my year 2000 version of chicken pot pie: big chunks of chicken (I really prefer thigh meat because it's moister) and pieces of chicken sausage for more flavor. I always like the texture of biscuits on top of the pie instead of a pie crust, and a biscuit topping is simpler to do.

FILLING

12	ounces Italian-style chicken sausage, casings removed
1	tablespoon oil
6	cups rich homemade chicken stock
1¹/₂	cups pearl onions, peeled
3	tablespoons clarified butter
1¹/₂	pounds fresh shiitake mushrooms, stemmed and quartered
4	tablespoons butter
2	cups coarsely chopped onion
³/₄	cup flour
¹/₂	cup heavy whipping cream

Salt

Freshly ground black pepper

6	cups cubed Roast Chicken (page 147)
1¹/₂	cups ³/₈-inch diagonally-sliced celery
¹/₂	cup chopped fresh parsley

1. To prepare the filling, place the chicken sausage in a bowl. Using a heaping tablespoon of the sausage, form balls in the palm of your hand. Repeat until you have used all the sausage.

2. Line a plate with paper towels. In a skillet over medium-high heat, add the oil. Cook the sausage balls in batches until cooked through. Drain the sausage on the plate and set aside.

3. In a small saucepan over medium-high heat, bring the chicken stock to a boil. Add the pearl onions and cook for 5 minutes until just cooked through. Using a slotted spoon, transfer the onions to a plate and set aside. Reserve the stock.

4. In a sauté pan over high heat, add the clarified butter. When the butter is sizzling hot, add the mushrooms and quickly sauté until the mushrooms are browned without releasing any juices. Transfer to a plate and set aside.

5. In a 4-quart, oven-proof Dutch oven, melt the butter and add the chopped onions. Cook until translucent, approximately 10 to 12 minutes. Add the flour and using a whisk, stir constantly for 2 minutes to cook the flour. Add the reserved chicken stock slowly, stirring continuously until all the stock is blended into the flour, and cook until the mixture thickens. Add the cream and cook for another 2 minutes. Season with salt and pepper. Add the sausage balls, pearl onions, mushrooms, chicken, celery, and parsley to the sauce and mix well. Remove from the heat.

6. Preheat the oven to 350 degrees F.

HERB BISCUIT TOPPING

2	**cups flour, sifted**
1	**tablespoon baking powder**
1	**teaspoon salt**
1	**tablespoon chopped fresh tarragon**
1/3	**cup butter, chilled and cut into small cubes**
3/4	**cup milk**

7. To prepare the biscuit topping, in a food processor, place the flour, baking powder, and salt. Pulse twice to mix the dry ingredients together. Add the tarragon and the butter to the bowl. Pulse until the mixture looks like cornmeal. With the machine running, add the milk through the feed tube, and as soon as the mixture becomes a smooth dough, turn off the machine.

8. Turn the dough out onto a floured board. Knead lightly a few times. Roll or pat the dough into 1/2-inch thickness. Cut out rounds with a biscuit cutter. (You could use refrigerated biscuits or a premade pie crust from the supermarket instead of making your own.)

9. Top the pie with the biscuits and bake for 30 minutes. Remove from the oven and serve.

Serves 6

ingredient note: *Clarified butter is butter that has been melted and strained of the milk solids. To make it, melt butter in a saucepan. As it melts, you will notice the milk solids that separate from the clear liquid. When the butter has melted and slightly cooled, pour it through a very fine-mesh strainer or a coffee filter, straining the liquid from the milk solids. Discard the milk solids; the clear butter that is left has been clarified.*

mexican chicken enchilada casserole

When I was growing up, our family ventured out to the Spanish Village restaurant for Mexican food. I always ordered the club sandwich or hamburger until I was about twelve or thirteen years old. Then I moved on to tacos. I was never a fan of Mexican food; I just wasn't a fan of spicy food. But then my palate changed and I began to love spices, peppers, and hot foods. As the years went on, I made Mexican-style casseroles and this recipe is the evolution of what is now a favorite food.

ENCHILADA SAUCE

1/2	tablespoon chili powder
1	tablespoon cumin seeds, toasted and ground
2	teaspoons garlic granules or flakes
2	teaspoons dried oregano
1	pinch cinnamon
2	teaspoons cocoa powder
6	tablespoons Wondra flour
10	cups chicken stock
2	cups tomato sauce
1	teaspoon salt

ENCHILADAS

3	cups cubed Roast Chicken meat (page 147)
2	cups garbanzo beans, cooked
2	cups black beans, cooked
2	cups fresh corn kernels
1	cup finely chopped red onion
1	cup black olives, sliced
1	cup chopped fresh cilantro leaves
1	tablespoon finely minced garlic

Salt

Freshly ground black pepper

1 1/2	cups grated Monterey Jack cheese
1 1/2	cups grated sharp Cheddar cheese
2	dozen corn tortillas

1. To prepare the sauce, in a saucepan, add the chili powder, cumin, garlic, oregano, cinnamon, cocoa powder, and Wondra. With a wooden spoon, mix the ingredients together well. Using a whisk, slowly add 6 cups of the chicken stock and blend. Place the saucepan over medium-high heat and, stirring constantly, heat until the mixture thickens. Add the tomato sauce and salt, blend well, and heat through. Remove from the heat and set aside.

2. Preheat the oven to 350 degrees F. Grease a 9 by 13-inch deep baking dish.

3. In a saucepan over medium-high heat, heat the remaining 4 cups of chicken stock. Keep warm.

4. In a large mixing bowl, combine the chicken, garbanzo beans, black beans, corn, onion, olives, 1/2 cup of the cilantro, and garlic. Season with salt and pepper.

5. In a medium mixing bowl, combine the cheeses.

6. To assemble, dip each corn tortilla into the warm chicken stock. Layer 6 tortillas in the bottom of the baking dish, overlapping the edges. Cover the tortillas with one-third of the chicken and bean mixture. Ladle about 1 to 1 1/2 cups of the tomato–spice sauce over the mixture and sprinkle one-quarter of the cheese over the top of sauce. Repeat two more times ending with a layer of tortillas. Pour 2 cups of the sauce over the tortillas and sprinkle with the remaining cheese.

7. Place the casserole in the oven and bake for 30 to 45 minutes until bubbly on top. Remove from the oven and let stand for 5 minutes before serving.

continued on page 94

1   **cup sour cream, for garnish**

2   **teaspoons freshly squeezed lime juice, for garnish**

2   **cups seeded and coarsely chopped tomatoes, for garnish**

1   **cup pumpkin seeds, roasted and salted, for garnish**

8. In a small bowl, mix the sour cream and lime juice. Transfer to a serving bowl. In another small bowl, mix the tomatoes and the remaining $1/2$ cup cilantro. Transfer to a serving bowl. Serve as garnishes for casserole along with the pumpkin seeds.

Serves 8

ingredient note: *Toasting whole spices then grinding them results in more flavor and aroma than using ground spices out of a jar. To do this, simply place whole spices like cumin in a small skillet over medium heat. Toast, shaking the pan, until the spice is fragrant. Remove from the heat, transfer the spice to a spice grinder (a small coffee grinder is ideal), and grind to a powder. Prepare only as much as you need for best flavor. Find whole spices at natural food stores or online.*

leftovers? You're likely to have extra enchilada sauce, but it will keep in an airtight container in the refrigerator for 2 weeks. Or freeze it for your next batch of enchilada casserole. Use this sauce in other dishes, too, like burritos, chile rellenos, and over roast pork or grilled chicken.

new wave tuna-noodle casserole

How do you take a classic dish and make it part of the contemporary food scene in Hawai'i? Well, first you start with fresh tuna instead of canned; it would be sacrilegious to do otherwise. Then you add the flavors from our mostly Asian community and you come up with a dish that says, "This is Hawai'i Regional Cuisine today," a dish that goes to a whole new level of delicious flavor.

PANKO-PEA MIXTURE

3	tablespoons butter
1/2	cup panko flakes (Japanese bread crumbs)
1/2	cup wasabi peas, crushed

MUSHROOM MIXTURE

2	tablespoons butter
1	cup thinly sliced onions
1/2	pound fresh shiitake mushrooms, stems removed and cut into thirds
2	teaspoons finely minced garlic
1	tablespoon finely minced fresh ginger
1	cup 1/4-inch slices baby corn
1/2	cup sliced and halved water chestnuts
1/2	cup edamame (soybeans)

SAUCE

3	tablespoons butter
3	tablespoons flour
3	cups chicken stock, at room temperature
3	cups half-and-half, at room temperature
4	tablespoons oyster sauce
2	teaspoons Sriracha (Thai chile sauce)
3	teaspoons fish sauce
3	teaspoons fresh lime juice
1	cup coarsely chopped cilantro

1. Preheat the oven to 350 degrees F. Generously grease a 9 by 13-inch casserole dish.

2. To make the panko-pea mixture, in a large sauté pan over medium-high heat, melt the butter. Add the panko flakes and crushed wasabi peas and toast to golden brown, stirring. Transfer to a bowl and set aside.

3. To prepare the mushroom mixture, in the same pan over medium heat, add the butter. Add the onions and cook until soft, about 4 minutes, stirring occasionally. Increase the heat to medium-high and add the mushrooms, cooking until the mushroom liquid evaporates, stirring often. Add the garlic, ginger, corn, water chestnuts, and edamame and cook 1 minute. Remove from heat and set aside.

4. To prepare the sauce, in a saucepan over medium heat, melt the 3 tablespoons of butter. When the butter starts to foam, add the flour and blend together with a wire whisk; cook for 3 minutes, stirring. Add the chicken stock and the half-and-half in a slow steady stream, whisking continuously. Add the oyster sauce, Sriracha, fish sauce, and lime juice. Add the mushroom mixture, 1/2 cup chopped cilantro and stir well. Remove from the heat and set aside.

continued on page 98

TUNA AND NOODLES

1	pound egg noodles
1¹/₂	pounds fresh tuna, cut into 1-inch steaks
2	tablespoons oil

Salt

Freshly ground black pepper

5. In a large pot of boiling salted water, cook the noodles about 8 to 10 minutes, or until just al dente. Strain the noodles in a fine-mesh strainer and transfer the noodles to a large bowl. Add the mushroom mixture and toss well to incorporate. Pour the mixture into the casserole dish. Cover with foil and place on a baking sheet and into the oven. Bake for 20 minutes, or until heated through.

6. To prepare the tuna, while the casserole is cooking, generously season the tuna with salt and pepper. In a large nonstick sauté pan over high heat, add 2 tablespoons oil and sear the tuna for 30 seconds on each side. The tuna should still be very rare. Transfer to a cutting board and slice the tuna steaks into ¹/₂-inch thick slices.

7. When the casserole is ready, remove it from the oven. Place the tuna slices on the top of the noodles, overlapping the slices. Cover with the panko-wasabi pea mixture and return the casserole to the oven for 5 minutes. Remove from the oven, sprinkle with remaining cilantro, and serve.

Serves 6

smoked salmon lasagna

This is one of the first recipes I ever made up. It became a signature dish, and we still serve it for holiday brunch buffets. It's perfect for brunch, lunch, or dinner with a fresh green salad.

1/2 cup, plus 3 tablespoons butter

1/2 cup flour

3 cups milk

3 cups half-and-half

3/4 cup (about 2 ounces) crumbled soft herb cheese (such as Boursin or Rondele)

2 teaspoons salt

1 teaspoon white pepper

3/4 cup oil-packed sun-dried tomatoes, drained and julienned

3/4 pound cremini mushrooms, thinly sliced

Freshly ground black pepper

Salt

1 pound spinach lasagna noodles

2 tablespoons olive oil

2 pounds sliced smoked salmon

12 hard-cooked eggs, each sliced into 4 round slices

1 1/2 cups shredded Parmigiano-Reggiano cheese

2 tablespoons finely chopped fresh chives, for garnish

1. Preheat the oven to 350 degrees F.

2. To make the sauce, in a 2-quart saucepan over medium-high heat, melt 1/2 cup of butter. Add the flour and stir with a whisk; cook for 3 minutes, stirring constantly. Remove the saucepan from the heat and slowly add the milk and the half-and-half, stirring constantly to avoid lumps. Return the saucepan to the burner over low heat. Stirring constantly, allow the sauce to thicken. Add the herb cheese and stir to incorporate. Add the 2 teaspoons of salt and white pepper and stir. Remove from the heat and set aside.

3. In a small pot of simmering water, add the sun-dried tomatoes and simmer until the tomatoes soften, about 5 minutes. Drain the tomatoes and set aside in a small bowl.

4. In a large sauté pan over high heat, melt the remaining 3 tablespoons of butter. Add the mushrooms and sauté quickly to brown the mushrooms. Season with salt and black pepper. Transfer the mushrooms to a colander to drain and set aside.

5. In a large pot of salted boiling water, add the lasagna noodles and cook for 5 minutes. Drain into a colander and rinse with cold water. Drizzle the noodles with olive oil to keep them separated.

6. Grease a 9 by 13-inch deep casserole dish with olive oil. Ladle 1 cup of sauce into the bottom of the dish. Cover the sauce with a layer of noodles. Cover the noodles with 1/2 cup of sauce. Layer one third of the salmon slices over the noodles. Sprinkle one third of the tomatoes, mushrooms, and eggs evenly over the salmon. Sprinkle the mixture with 1/3 cup of the cheese. Ladle 1 cup of the sauce over the salmon mixture. Repeat the process starting with the noodles and form two more layers. Finish with a layer of noodles. Cover the final layer of noodles with the remaining sauce and cheese.

7. Place the lasagna in the oven and bake for 45 to 60 minutes, or until hot, bubbly, and brown on top. Remove from the oven, sprinkle with chopped chives and serve.

Serves 8

truffle macaroni and cheese

When the retro food trend happened a few years ago, macaroni and cheese was the first thing I thought of to bring back. But, of course, I had to get a little more creative and make it a little different. Voilà! To make this the ultimate decadent macaroni and cheese dish, add 2½ cups of cubed not-quite-cooked-through lobster meat to the pasta and sauce. To die for!

6	tablespoons butter
¼	cup sliced onion
1	tablespoon coarsely chopped shallot
1	clove garlic, smashed
½	teaspoon whole black peppercorns
3½	cups heavy cream
3	cups half-and-half
2	tablespoons flour
1½	cups grated sharp white Cheddar cheese
½	cup grated fontina cheese
½	cup grated Parmigiano-Reggiano cheese

Salt

Freshly ground white pepper

1½	pounds penne pasta
1	cup panko (Japanese breadcrumbs)
1	tablespoon chopped fresh chives
1	tablespoon chopped fresh parsley
3	tablespoons truffle oil

1. In a saucepan over medium heat, melt 1 tablespoon of the butter. Add the onion, shallot, and garlic and cook for two minutes or until the onion wilts. Add the peppercorns, the heavy cream, and the half-and-half. Decrease the heat to low and simmer for 10 minutes. Remove the cream mixture from the heat and carefully strain the mixture through a fine strainer into a bowl with a pouring spout. Discard the vegetables.

2. In the same saucepan over medium high heat, melt 3 tablespoons of the butter. Add the flour and whisk into the butter. Continue to stir, cooking the mixture for 2 minutes or until the flour changes color from white to beige. Slowly add the cream mixture, whisking constantly. Continue to cook and stir until the mixture thickens, about 5 minutes. Remove from the heat. Add the Cheddar, fontina, and Parmigiano-Reggiano cheeses and stir, blending the cheeses into the sauce. Season with salt and pepper. Set aside.

3. Preheat the oven to 325 degrees F. Grease an ovenproof casserole dish.

4. In a large pot of boiling salted water, cook the pasta about 8 to 10 minutes until al dente.

5. While the pasta is cooking, in a sauté pan over medium-high heat, melt the remaining 2 tablespoons of the butter. Add the panko and sauté until the panko is golden brown, about 3 minutes. Remove the pan from the heat and add the parsley and chives and mix together.

6. When the pasta is cooked to just al dente, drain it and save ½ cup of the pasta water. Transfer the pasta into a large bowl and pour the sauce over the pasta. With a wooden spoon, incorporate the sauce into the pasta, making sure the sauce gets into the tubes of pasta. If the sauce is too thick, add a few tablespoons of the pasta water to thin.

continued on page 102

ingredient note: *Truffle oil is an ingredient worth having in your pantry. Even though it doesn't contain real truffles, the rare and expensive fungus prized by gourmands, it does infuse its pungent, earthy aroma into dishes in a wonderful way. Drizzle it over mashed potatoes, risotto, soups; use it sparingly but to good effect.*

7. Pour the pasta into the casserole dish. Top with the panko mixture. Place the casserole in the oven for 12 to 15 minutes, or until heated through. Remove from the oven, and with a knife poke holes all over the casserole from top to bottom. Drizzle the truffle oil over the top through the holes. Let sit for 2 minutes and serve.

Serves 8

artichoke-spinach casserole

The first cookbook I ever read was the *Dallas Junior League Cookbook*. This recipe, which I've changed over the years to suit my taste, was in it. Fresh spinach, for example, makes it better than using frozen spinach as in the original recipe. This casserole is very easy to make and at the end of a meal, it's the dish everyone talks about. Serve it alongside anything you cook on the grill.

15	tablespoons butter, at room temperature
2	pounds fresh baby spinach
1	(8-ounce) package cream cheese, at room temperature
1/2	cup sliced water chestnuts, then halved

Salt

Freshly ground black pepper

1	cup panko (Japanese breadcrumbs)
2	cups quartered frozen artichoke hearts

leftovers? You'll hardly ever have any, but just in case, you can put the leftovers in a food processor, add a dollop of sour cream and/or mayonnaise and blend it until smooth. Then serve it with chips or crackers as a dip!

1. Preheat the oven to 350 degrees F.

2. Grease a 1 1/2-quart shallow baking dish.

3. In a large sauté pan over medium heat, melt 3 tablespoons of the butter. Add the spinach and cook until wilted. Transfer the spinach to a fine-mesh sieve. Using the back of a spoon, squeeze out the excess moisture.

4. On a cutting board using a sharp knife, coarsely chop the spinach. Return the spinach to the sauté pan and over low heat, add the cream cheese and 8 tablespoons of the butter. Stir constantly and mix all the ingredients together. Add the water chestnuts, season with salt and pepper, and mix well. Remove from the heat.

5. In a medium sauté pan over medium heat, melt 2 tablespoons of butter. Add the panko and sauté for 3 to 5 minutes or until golden brown. Transfer to a bowl and set aside.

6. In the same sauté pan over medium heat, melt the remaining 2 tablespoons of butter. Add the artichoke hearts and cook for 2 minutes. Transfer the artichoke hearts to the baking dish, spreading them evenly over the bottom. Spread the spinach mixture evenly over the artichokes. Top with the panko. Place the baking dish in the oven and bake for 30 to 40 minutes.

Serves 8

ingredient note: *Panko is prepackaged Japanese breadcrumbs sold in Asian food stores and many supermarkets. The breadcrumbs are usually coarse (there is also a fine version) and become very crunchy when fried. They are a terrific topping for casseroles, and if you're ever in need of breadcrumbs for meat loaf or crab cakes, panko works too!*

shiitake mushroom bread pudding

Every year at Thanksgiving, we try to come up with a new dish—a stuffing or a starch—for the hundreds of customers who dine with us at the restaurants. This is one of those dishes, something with a little Asian flavor from the herbs and the shiitake mushrooms. This dish has the flavor of a really great mushroom soup, except you eat it with a fork.

2	pounds fresh shiitake mushrooms
3	tablespoons butter
3	tablespoons olive oil
1	tablespoon minced shallots
6	cups half-and-half
1	tablespoon finely chopped garlic
1	tablespoon finely chopped fresh ginger
1	tablespoon finely chopped lemongrass
2	tablespoons chiffonade of fresh basil

Salt

Freshly ground black pepper

6	eggs
1/4	cup, plus 1 tablespoon grated Parmigiano-Reggiano cheese
1/2	cup grated fontina cheese
3/4	teaspoon salt
1/2	teaspoon ground white pepper
6	cups crustless 1-inch cubes sourdough bread
1	tablespoon chopped chives, for garnish

1. Lightly grease a 3-quart casserole dish.

2. Remove the stems from the mushrooms and set aside. Slice half of the mushroom caps into thirds and set aside. Place the stems and the remaining half of the mushroom caps in a food processor with the metal blade. Process until finely chopped.

3. In a large sauté pan over high heat, melt 1 tablespoon of butter with 1 tablespoon of oil. Add the chopped mushrooms and shallots and sauté until lightly browned, about 5 minutes. Add the half-and-half and bring to a boil. Decrease the heat to low and simmer for 10 to 12 minutes. Remove from the heat and cool. Strain the liquid into a bowl using a fine-mesh strainer, pressing on the mushrooms to extract all the liquid. Cool the liquid and set aside. Discard the mushrooms.

4. In a large sauté pan over medium-high heat, add 1 tablespoon of the butter and 1 tablespoon of oil. Add half of the sliced mushrooms and cook for 3 to 4 minutes. Transfer the mushrooms to a bowl and repeat with the remaining butter, oil, and mushrooms. Return all the mushrooms to the sauté pan and add the garlic, ginger, lemongrass, and basil and cook for 1 minute, stirring to blend. Season with salt and pepper. Drain any liquid in the pan into a small cup. Set mushroom mixture aside to cool.

5. In a large bowl, whisk together the eggs and the mushroom-infused half-and-half. Add 1/4 cup Parmigiano-Reggiano and fontina cheeses, salt, and pepper. Add the bread cubes and let stand for 15 to 20 minutes allowing the bread to soak up the liquid.

6. Preheat the oven to 350 degrees F.

7. Stir in the mushroom mixture into the egg–bread mixture, and mix well. Pour into the baking dish. Bake until lightly browned and puffy, approximately 1 hour. Remove from the oven and sprinkle with the remaining tablespoon of Parmigiano-Reggiano cheese and the chives.

Serves 8

ingredient note: *Panko is prepackaged Japanese breadcrumbs sold in Asian food stores and many supermarkets. The breadcrumbs are usually coarse (there is also a fine version) and become very crunchy when fried. They are a terrific topping for casseroles, and if you're ever in need of breadcrumbs for meat loaf or crab cakes, panko works too!*

potato-plum casserole

There's nothing like a creamy potato casserole with a layer of dried plums. Okay, they are prunes, and it may not sound like a terrific combination but trust me—it is.

2   tablespoons butter

1   cup ¼-inch sliced leeks, white part only

1½ cups dried plums, cut into quarters

3   cups heavy whipping cream

1   cup chicken stock

5   pounds Yukon gold potatoes

Salt

Freshly ground black pepper

1. In a sauté pan over medium-high heat, melt the butter. Add the leeks and sauté for 4 minutes, or until soft; do not allow to brown. Add the plums and cook for 2 minutes. Remove the pan from the heat and set aside to cool.

2. In a saucepan over medium heat, warm the cream and chicken stock together. Keep warm.

3. Preheat the oven to 350 degrees F.

4. Grease a 9 by 13-inch casserole. Peel the potatoes and slice ⅛-inch thick on a mandoline. Quickly layer the potato slices into the casserole dish, seasoning each layer with salt and pepper. When half of the dish is filled with the potatoes, add enough of the cream and chicken stock mixture to cover the potatoes.

5. Make a layer with the leeks and dried plums and press down into the dish. Continue to layer and season the potatoes until they fill the casserole dish, leaving room for the remaining liquid. Cover the potatoes with the rest of the liquid. Place the casserole into the oven and bake for 40 to 50 minutes until cooked through.

Serves 8

ingredient note: *Yukon gold potatoes are a golden-skinned tuber with a light yellow flesh. Their creamy texture makes these potatoes excellent for mashing, and they hold up well in soups and chowders. Their starchiness makes them perfect for this layered casserole. If you cannot find Yukon golds, a good russet will do.*

noodle kugel

This classic Jewish recipe for noodle pudding is a family one, passed down through the genera-
tions. We always had this during the holidays, a time when aunts and uncles descended on our
home to share a meal. At our house, Noodle Kugel was always served as a side dish with brisket or
other meats, the sweetness balancing the savoriness of entrées.

8	ounces egg noodles
6	tablespoons butter, melted
12	ounces ricotta cheese
6	large eggs, beaten
2	cups sweetened applesauce
3/4	cup raisins
1	teaspoon cinnamon
1/2	teaspoon pure vanilla extract
1/2	cup toasted and chopped pecans

1. Preheat the oven to 350 degrees F.

2. Grease a 9 by 13-inch baking dish.

3. In a pot of boiling salted water, cook the noodles until just al dente,
about 6 minutes. Drain the noodles in a colander and return them to the
pot. Toss with the melted butter.

4. In a large mixing bowl, blend together the ricotta cheese and eggs. Add
the applesauce, raisins, cinnamon, and vanilla and mix well. Add the
noodles and toss to coat the noodles with the cheese mixture. Transfer
the noodles to the baking dish.

5. Bake for 30 minutes, or until set. Sprinkle the pecans over the top
and serve.

Serves 6

Beef, Pork, and Lamb

I AM A HARDCORE CARNIVORE.

I was raised on beef and love it. I remember fillets so tender and juicy that you could cut them with a fork. I totally remember the taste of well-marbled New York steaks my mother used to buy at Cabell's Mini Mart, a little market close to home. And when Mom cooked sirloin steaks, she would cook one for every person at the table and there wasn't much left over.

I still love beef and I've always cooked prime rib, tenderloin, and steak. In my restaurants, people still eat beef, second only to fresh fish. In my mind, there's nothing better than steak and eggs in the morning or a slice of cold tenderloin left over from the night before. Long live eating beef!

I'm also a big fan of pork. It's a meat that has been misunderstood for too long. People have always felt that it had to be cooked well done. There's nothing better than pork tenderloin, cut into pieces and pounded like scaloppine and cooked quickly until just done, keeping its moisture and tenderness. Pork roasts are a particular favorite, made with a pork butt that has lots of fat in it so when you cook it, it's always tender and moist.

In Hawai'i, whole pigs cooked in an *imu* (underground oven lined with hot stones) is the best party food. On New Year's Eve, I often cater parties where the centerpiece is the kālua (roasted) pork out of the *imu*. But I rarely get to eat it because I'm cooking. So the next morning, my treat is kālua pork warmed in the microwave, stacked in a Hawaiian sweet bread roll, and a big glass of milk. It's my antidote to too much champagne the night before.

Another favorite pork preparation is a spit-roasted pig, where it is slowly turned over an open fire so that the fat drips away and the skin gets crunchy and crisp. It's better than any *chicharrón* you'll ever eat.

When I was growing up, lamb at our house meant leg of lamb and lamb shanks—especially lamb shanks because my dad loved them. My mom would look for the meatiest shanks at the supermarket and buy two or three at a time and store them in the freezer until she had gathered at least a dozen of them. Then she would cook them, and my dad would eat six or eight of them at a sitting. He'd clean the bones; it was amazing to watch.

Beef, pork, lamb—love to cook and eat them all. Next time you're having a family celebration at home, consider cooking a big prime rib roast, leg of lamb, or pork roast. It's festive and comforting food, and the best part is you'll have leftovers to make two or three more meals!

Beef, Pork, and Lamb

joe's favorite meatloaf

When I was thinking about doing a second restaurant, I thought about comfort food—and there's nothing more homey and comforting than meatloaf. This meatloaf has been on the menu of Joe's in Wailea since day one, and I even put it on the coach menu for Hawaiian Airlines where it got rave reviews. Now this recipe makes a lot of meatloaf, but at my house it would be all gone in one meal. At the restaurant, we serve meatloaf in twelve-ounce portions—believe me it all gets eaten!

5	pounds lean ground beef
1	cup peeled, minced carrot
1/3	cup minced celery
1	cup minced onion
1 1/3	cups Hali'imaile Barbecue Sauce, plus additional sauce (page 14)
1	teaspoon freshly ground black pepper
1	tablespoon salt
1	teaspoon finely chopped fresh thyme
5	cloves garlic, minced
6	eggs

1. Preheat the oven to 350 degrees F.

2. To prepare the meatloaf, place the ground beef in a large mixing bowl and break it apart. Add all the remaining ingredients and mix well. Form 2 loaves (or any other shape you like) and place in an ungreased baking dish. Baste with a bit more barbecue sauce, and bake for 45 minutes.

3. To serve, heat extra barbecue sauce to ladle over each serving of meatloaf.

Serves at least 6, very generously

leftovers? Make meatloaf sandwiches, thick slices on good sandwich bread, slathered with mayonnaise and ketchup.

bev's world-famous chili revealed!

I served this chili one night at a party that included industrialist Lee Iacocca. He came up to me and said, "I've been a spokesman for one thing in my life [Chrysler]; if you want, I'll be a spokesman for this chili." I've been making this chili for thirty years. It's a simple chili, but no matter how much I make, it all disappears. It's the one thing I have to make whenever I visit my grandkids.

4	tablespoons oil
2¹/₂	cups chopped onions
5	cloves garlic, minced
5	pounds ground beef (10% fat)
¹/₂	cup chili powder
Salt	
Freshly ground black pepper	
2	tablespoons chipotle chile powder
2	(28-ounce) cans tomato sauce
2	(28-ounce) cans diced canned tomatoes
2	tablespoons ground cumin
1	tablespoon dried oregano
1	cup sour cream, for garnish
1	cup grated sharp Cheddar cheese, for garnish
1	cup chopped Maui onions or other sweet onion, for garnish
¹/₂	cup chopped fresh cilantro leaves, for garnish

1. In a large stockpot over medium-high heat, add 1 tablespoon of the oil. Add the onions and garlic and cook until the onions are wilted, about 8 to 10 minutes. Remove from the heat and set aside.

2. In a large sauté pan over medium-high heat, add 1 tablespoon of the oil. In batches, crumble the ground beef into the pan and cook, breaking the meat into small pieces. Sprinkle each batch with 1 tablespoon of the chili powder, season with salt and pepper, and stir to mix well. Add more oil as needed to cook the rest of the beef. When all the meat has been cooked, add the remaining chili powder and the chipotle chile powder. Transfer the beef to the pot with the onions.

3. Over medium heat, cook the beef-onion mixture, stirring to blend well. Add the tomato sauce and blend well. Add the diced tomatoes with juice and blend well. Lower the heat and simmer the chili for 2 hours, stirring frequently. Add the cumin and the oregano; season with salt and pepper and cook for 20 minutes more.

4. Serve the chili accompanied by the sour cream, cheese, onions, and cilantro.

Serves 8

leftovers? Fill an omelet with chili, top with sour cream, cheese, onions, and cilantro. Serve chili over spinach enchiladas. Make chili wontons. Last but not least, freeze the chili in small containers for a quick meal.

hoisin-marinated short ribs and wasabi mashed potatoes

A few years ago, as beef prices started to climb, I started looking at cuts other than fillets, rib-eyes, and New York steaks. And as I started working for Hawaiian Airlines, I realized I needed cuts of meat that could be cooked ahead and reheated. Since I love braised meats—they're second only to a great steak—I went directly to short ribs. Of course I wanted an Asian flavor in my short ribs and the robust flavor you get when you braise with a good beef stock.

SHORT RIBS

6	pounds boneless beef short ribs, cut into 6-ounce portions

Salt

Freshly ground black pepper

2	tablespoons Chinese Five-Spice Powder (page 13)
4	tablespoons oil
1¹/₂ cups chopped onions
1	tablespoon finely minced fresh ginger
4	cloves garlic, finely minced
2	stalks lemongrass, coarsely chopped
¹/₄	cup firmly packed brown sugar
12	cups beef stock
1	cup hoisin sauce (Chinese sweet spicy sauce)
1	cup sliced green onions, for garnish

WASABI MASHED POTATOES

2	tablespoons wasabi powder
3	tablespoons water
6	tablespoons butter, at room temperature
6	large baking potatoes, peeled and cubed
3	tablespoons milk

Salt

Freshly ground white pepper

1. Preheat the oven to 350 degrees F.

2. To prepare the short ribs, with a paper towel, pat the short rib pieces to remove moisture. In a small bowl, mix together the salt, pepper, and five-spice powder. Season the short ribs with this mixture.

3. Place a heavy Dutch oven or wide stockpot with a lid over high heat and add 2 tablespoons of the oil. When the oil is hot, add the short ribs in batches, cooking until all sides are browned. Transfer the short ribs to a plate and set aside.

4. Add the remaining 2 tablespoons of oil to the pot and add the onions. Cook for 2 minutes. Add the ginger, garlic, lemon grass, and brown sugar and cook until the onions become translucent, about 4 minutes.

5. Add the beef stock and stir. Add the short ribs and move them around until the ribs are covered in liquid. Place the lid on the pot and place the pot in the oven. Cook the short ribs for 2¹/₂ hours, or until fork tender.

6. Remove the pot from the oven and remove the short ribs to an oven-proof dish, leaving the braising liquid in the pot. Set the short ribs aside and keep warm. Keep the oven on.

7. Ladle any fat off the top of the braising liquid. Stir in the hoisin sauce. Over medium-high heat, reduce the braising liquid by half. Strain the sauce through a fine-mesh strainer and pour the sauce over the short ribs, coating the ribs well. Cover and place the short ribs in the oven to heat through. While short ribs are heating, prepare the wasabi butter and potatoes.

continued on page 116

leftovers? To make Asian tacos, remove the meat from the bones and shred. Heat with any remaining sauce and fill soft or crisp tortillas.

8. To make the wasabi butter, mix the wasabi powder with 2 tablespoons of the water in a small bowl. Stir to make a paste, adding the rest of the water as needed. Let the mixture rest for 5 to 8 minutes. Add the softened butter and blend well.

9. To prepare the potatoes, place them in a large pot with water to cover and bring to a boil over medium-high heat. Cook for 15 minutes, or until tender. Drain the liquid and transfer the potatoes to a bowl. Mash the potatoes with a potato masher, then add the milk and the wasabi butter. Continue mashing until the mixture is smooth. Season with salt and pepper.

10. Serve the short ribs garnished with green onions and accompanied by Wasabi Mashed Potatoes.

Serves 6

ingredient notes: *Chinese five-spice powder is a powdery blend of star anise, cinnamon, Szechuan peppercorns, fennel, and cloves, often used as a seasoning with meats and poultry or, with salt added, as a dipping condiment. To make your own, see page 13.*

Wasabi is Japanese horseradish, light green in color and packing a pungent bite. It's rarely available fresh; wasabi powder is commonly used, mixed with water to form a paste. The powder is really horseradish and coloring. A paste version is also available in some markets.

braised oxtails

Living in Hawai'i, I'd always see oxtails on menus, especially oxtail soup and stew. It kind of horrified me—oooh, oxtails! But a few years ago when I was shopping at the supermarket, I saw a package of oxtails and said, "Let's see what this is all about." So I made oxtails with a tomato sauce: it was the best thing I ever put in my mouth. The fatty, tender meat was so good. Oxtails have become one of my favorite things to eat, and I love to suck the meat off the bones. The only thing that makes this dish better is to make it a day ahead of the day you want to eat it.

4	pounds oxtails, cut into 2-inch thick pieces
1	cup flour
2	tablespoons salt
1	tablespoon freshly ground black pepper
4	tablespoons olive oil
2	cups finely chopped onion
5	cloves garlic, peeled and crushed
2	cups homemade beef stock, or good-quality canned broth
2	cups red wine
4	cups tomato sauce
8	sprigs fresh thyme
2	bay leaves
4	carrots, peeled and sliced into 1/2-inch pieces
3	ribs celery, trimmed and sliced diagonally into 1/2-inch pieces
2	medium leeks, trimmed, rinsed, and cut into 1/2-inch rounds

1. To prepare the oxtails, rinse the oxtail pieces in water and pat dry. In a mixing bowl, mix the flour, 1 tablespoon of the salt, and 1 teaspoon of the pepper. Season the oxtails with the remaining salt and pepper, then coat the pieces of oxtail in the flour mixture.

2. In a large heavy braising pan over medium-high heat, add 3 tablespoons of the olive oil. When the oil is hot, add the oxtails in batches, turning to brown all sides. Transfer the oxtails to a plate. Add the remaining 1 tablespoon of olive oil to the pan. Add the onions and garlic and cook, stirring constantly, until they soften and begin to turn translucent, about 4 minutes. Return the oxtails to the pan.

3. Add the stock and the wine and stir, scraping up any browned bits from the bottom of the pan. Add the tomato sauce, thyme, and bay leaves. Stir well, cover, and bring to a boil. Decrease the heat to low, cover, and simmer until the meat is tender, about 2 hours.

4. Add the carrots, celery, and leeks to the oxtails, stirring so they are completely covered in sauce. Cover, and continue cooking until the vegetables are tender, about 30 minutes. Season with salt and pepper, and serve.

Serves 6

leftovers? Make oxtail raviolis. Remove the meat from the bones and coarsely chop. Add a little sauce from the oxtails to the meat. Moisten the edges of a wonton wrapper with beaten egg and place a generous tablespoon of meat in the center. Top with another wonton wrapper and press the edges firmly to seal. Cook in boiling water until raviolis float to the top. Serve with your favorite marinara sauce.

bev's beef brisket

My mother used to make beef brisket in one of those cooking bags: she would put the vegetables on the bottom, the brisket on top of them, sprinkle a packet of Lipton's onion soup mix over the beef, fill the bag with liquid, seal it, and cook it in the oven. The important things my mother taught me about cooking brisket were to keep it completely covered in liquid, cook it slowly, and leave it whole and with the fat on so the end product is tender and juicy. I've discarded the soup mix. Instead I use a good stock and some red wine for great flavor. Serve beef brisket with some roasted fingerling potatoes.

1	cup coarsely chopped onions
1	cup peeled and coarsely chopped carrots
1	cup coarsely chopped celery
8	shallots, cut in half
2	tablespoons minced garlic cloves
5	pounds whole beef brisket

Salt

Freshly ground black pepper

8	cups chicken or beef stock
1	cup red wine
6	fresh thyme sprigs
3	fresh rosemary sprigs

1. Preheat the oven to 325 degrees F.

2. In a deep roasting pan, add half of the chopped onions, carrots, and celery. Add the shallots and garlic to the pan. Season the brisket with salt and pepper. Place the brisket on top of the vegetables. Sprinkle the rest of the vegetables over the top of the brisket.

3. Pour the stock and the wine into the roasting pan; the liquid should completely cover the brisket. Cover the pan tightly with aluminum foil and place it in the oven. Roast for 3 hours, or until a knife easily pierces through the beef. When the beef is tender, transfer the beef to a platter.

4. To prepare the sauce, strain the remaining liquid through a fine-mesh sieve into a saucepan over medium-high heat, and reduce by half. Reserve the cooked vegetables. Place the saucepan over low heat; add the thyme and rosemary sprigs.

5. Place the cooked vegetables into a food processor and purée. Add the vegetable purée to the strained liquid and stir to blend. Cook for 6 to 8 minutes, or until the sauce is heated through.

6. Trim any fat off of the brisket and slice into 1/2-inch slices. Serve with the sauce.

Serves 6

leftovers? Shred the beef and mix it with Hali'imaile Barbecue Sauce (page 14) and make barbecue beef sandwiches. Mix shredded beef with black beans; spread on a tortilla, top with Cheddar cheese and lettuce, roll into a burrito. Scramble some eggs with Cheddar cheese, canned green chiles, and shredded beef for a breakfast scramble; serve with fresh tomato salsa.

fillet of beef *with grilled prosciutto-wrapped figs and fig demi-glace*

This is a special occasion dish—a dish to wow your family or friends with an incredible tasting fillet of beef. It also incorporates my favorite fruit: figs, fresh or dried. When figs are in season, a few friends with trees on Maui bring me their harvest. The figs end up in every dish on my menu; they're such a special treat!

FIGS

6	fresh figs, halved
6	slices prosciutto, halved

FIG DEMI-GLACE

1/2	cup diced dried figs
3/4	cup port wine
1	cup Demi-Glace (page 12)

BEEF

6	(8-ounce) fillets of beef

Salt

Freshly ground black pepper

2	tablespoons olive oil
3	tablespoons butter
3	teaspoons chopped garlic
2	pounds fresh baby spinach, stems removed
1	pound trumpet mushrooms, or other large fresh mushroom
2	teaspoons chopped fresh thyme leaves
1/2	pound blue cheese, crumbled

Fresh thyme sprigs, for garnish

1. Wrap the figs in the prosciutto slices. Place on a plate and set aside.

2. To prepare the fig demi-glace, in a small saucepan over low heat, add the dried figs and the port. Cook for 10 to 15 minutes, or until the port is reduced by half. Strain the liquid through a fine-mesh strainer into a small bowl, pressing on the figs to remove as much liquid as possible. Discard the figs.

3. In the same saucepan over low heat, warm the demi-glace and, with a wire whisk, blend in the fig-port liquid. Keep warm.

4. Preheat a gas or charcoal grill to medium-high heat.

5. To grill the beef and figs, season the fillets with salt and pepper. Brush the prosciutto-wrapped figs with 1 tablespoon of the olive oil. Place the figs on the grill, turning as each side gets grill marks. Place the fillets on the grill, and grill on each side for about 8 minutes for medium-rare doneness. Transfer the figs and fillets to a plate and keep warm.

6. To prepare the spinach, in a large sauté pan over medium-high heat, melt 2 tablespoons of the butter. Add 1 teaspoon of the garlic, then add the spinach and cook for 2 to 3 minutes until the spinach is wilted. Transfer the spinach to a plate and set aside in a warm place.

7. To prepare the mushrooms, in the same pan over high heat, add the remaining 1 tablespoon of butter and 1 tablespoon of olive oil. Then add the mushrooms and sauté until they begin to turn brown, about 6 minutes. Add the remaining 2 teaspoons of chopped garlic and the thyme and sauté until the mushrooms are golden brown.

continued on page 122

ingredient note: *Demi-glace, the reduction of veal stock, is a thick, syrupy liquid that becomes the basis for rich, flavorful sauces. To make your own, make a big pot of veal or beef stock, then reduce it down for hours and hours until you have a gelatinous liquid. If you'd like to give it a try, see page 12. Or beg some from a restaurant that makes it or buy a commercial equivalent, available in fine food stores.*

8. To serve, divide the spinach among 6 plates. Place 1 tablespoon of cheese over each spinach portion. Place the fillets on top of the spinach. Place the mushrooms and figs around each fillet. Pour ¼ cup of the fig demi-glace over each fillet. Garnish with fresh thyme and serve.

Serves 6

prime rib of beef *with horseradish sauce*

Over the years, I've learned that you get an amazing amount of flavor when you roast meat on the bone. When you buy a prime rib roast, have the butcher remove the meat from the bones, but save the whole rib piece and tie it onto the roast as it cooks. Not only will the bones add flavor, you'll have the bones for another great meal. Prime rib was one of my beef-night favorites when I was growing up, especially because it meant great leftovers. The horseradish sauce is a must, plus Shiitake Mushroom Bread Pudding (page 123).

1   (7- to 8-pound) standing rib roast, meat separated from the bones

$1/4$ cup salt

$1/4$ cup freshly ground black pepper

HORSERADISH SAUCE

2   cups sour cream

$1/4$ cup prepared horseradish

leftovers? For prime rib crostinis, place thinly sliced prime rib on a crisp slice of baguette and top with horseradish sauce. Make prime rib sandwiches! Or serve leftover prime rib slices on top of a salad. For the rib bones, cut the ribs into single pieces and reheat in Hali'imaile Barbecue Sauce (page 14).

1. Remove the roast and ribs from the refrigerator and bring to room temperature, about 1 hour.

2. Place an oven rack at the lowest part of the oven. Preheat the oven to 250 degrees F.

3. Rub the salt and pepper all over roast. Place the roast on the ribs and tie together with kitchen string in several laces. In a heavy roasting pan, place the roast, bone side down, fat side up,. Place the roast in the oven and cook for $2^{1}/_{2}$ hours. Check the temperature with a thermometer placed in the middle of the roast. For rare to medium rare, the thermometer should register 122 to 126 degrees F. Continue to cook until the desired temperature is reached.

4. When the roast is done, remove it from the oven and let it rest for 15 to 20 minutes. Untie the meat from the bones and place the roast on a platter to serve. Set the bones aside for another use.

5. To make the sauce, in a bowl, blend the horseradish and sour cream together.

6. Transfer to a serving bowl to serve with the roast.

Serves 8 to 10

ingredient note: *If you want to add flavor to your rib roast, age it for several days in your refrigerator. Remove the packaging and pat the roast dry with paper towels. Place the roast on a wire rack that sits on a paper towel-lined baking sheet. Place in the refrigerator for 4 to 5 days, uncovered. The point is to dry out the meat. When you are ready to cook it, remove the roast from the refrigerator and cut off any dried edges and fat. You will be amazed at how much more flavorful the meat becomes.*

jawaiian spiced pork *with portuguese sausage and cornbread dressing*

This dish, served mostly during the cooler winter months in upcountry Maui, gets lots of oohs and aahs when we serve it, especially because we finish it so that the skin is crispy. Everyone will say they can't possibly finish it, but after the meal, the plates are always clean except for the bone. I like the flavor of Kurobuta pork, raised in the United States. If you can find it, use it.

PORK

1   (5-pound) pork shoulder (picnic roast), bone in and skin on

1   tablespoon oil

Salt

Freshly ground black pepper

2   tablespoons Volcano Jawaiian Spice Blend

1   cup chopped fresh cilantro, for garnish

DRIED FRUIT COMPOTE

2   teaspoons olive oil

3   shallots, minced

1   cup apple juice

1   cup dried pears, cut into 1/4-inch dice

1   cup dried apricots, cut into 1/4-inch dice

1   cup dried cherries, cut into 1/4-inch dice

2   cups port wine

PORTUGUESE SAUSAGE AND CORNBREAD DRESSING

4   tablespoons butter

12 ounces Portuguese sausage, cut into 1/4-inch thick slices and halved

3   cups sliced fresh shiitake mushrooms, stems removed

Salt

Freshly ground black pepper

1. Preheat the oven to 350 degrees F.

2. To prepare the pork, in a roasting pan, coat the pork with the oil. Season with salt, pepper, and the spice blend. (You can do this 4 to 6 hours ahead and refrigerate the pork, allowing it to come to room temperature before roasting it.) Place the pork skin side up in the roasting pan. Put in the oven and roast for 3 to 3 1/2 hours, until the pork is tender and falling off the bone.

3. To make the compote, in a saucepan over medium-high heat, add the olive oil and the shallots. Cook for 2 minutes. Add the apple juice, the dried fruits, and the wine. Bring the mixture to a boil. Decrease the heat to a simmer. Cover and simmer for 30 minutes.

4. Remove the cover, increase the heat to medium and continue to cook for another 30 minutes or until the liquid evaporates and the mixture becomes a thick compote.

5. To prepare the dressing, generously grease a 9 by 13-inch ovenproof casserole.

6. In a large skillet over medium-high heat, melt 1 tablespoon of the butter. Add the sausage in batches and cook until lightly browned. Transfer the sausage to a large bowl and set aside.

7. To the same skillet, add 1 tablespoon of the butter and the mushrooms. Cook the mushrooms about 3 minutes, or until lightly browned. Season with salt and pepper. Transfer the mushrooms to the sausage bowl.

8. Decrease the heat to medium and in the same skillet, add the remaining 2 tablespoons of butter, lemongrass, onions, and celery. Cook for 3 minutes, or until the vegetables are just cooked. Stir in the green onions and macadamia nuts, and transfer the mixture to the sausage bowl. Add the cornbread to the bowl and toss together. Add the stock to moisten,

2   stalks lemongrass, finely minced

1   cup chopped onions

1   cup chopped celery

3/4 cups chopped green onions

3/4 cup toasted, coarsely chopped macadamia nuts

4   cups dried-out cornbread, coarsely crumbled

1   cup chicken stock

mixing well. Season with salt and pepper. Transfer the dressing to the casserole and cover with foil. Reheat for 20 to 25 minutes just before serving.

9. When the pork is done, remove it from the oven; leave the oven on. Pull off the skin and place it on a rimmed baking sheet. Return the skin to the oven and roast it for 30 to 45 minutes, or until it is brown and crisp. Remove from the oven and cool.

10. To serve, place a spoonful of cornbread dressing on a plate. Pull large chunks of meat from the roast and place it next to the stuffing. Ladle the compote alongside. Break pieces of the crispy skin onto the meat and serve.

Serves 6

ingredient notes: *Volcano Jawaiian Spice Blend is a jerk-style spice blend produced by Volcano Spice Company of Maui. To order, go to volcanospicecompany.com*

Kurobuta is the Japanese name for the Berkshire pig, a breed of pig originally from Britain that made its way to Japan. This black pig is appreciated for its tender, juicy, and well-marbled meat. American Kurobuta is raised on small family farms and is available through meat suppliers and specialty stores.

Portuguese sausage is a garlicky, spicy sausage that is renowned in Hawai'i and credited to the Portuguese immigrants who settled here. Linguiça would be a good substitute.

kālua pork and lobster spring rolls
with mango-chile dipping sauce

I'm always trying to come up with different spring rolls—they're something you expect to see in Hawai'i. Kālua pork, the traditional Hawaiian-roasted pork, smoky and succulent, is so good on its own, but it can be combined with so many other ingredients. This spring roll is wonderfully packed with all kinds of goodies—one batch will hardly be enough.

SPRING ROLLS

1	cup Kālua Pork (page 170)
1	cup chopped, cooked lobster
1	carrot, peeled and shredded
2	cups finely shredded won bok (Chinese or Napa cabbage)
6	green onions, white and green parts, finely chopped
3	cloves garlic, finely chopped
1	tablespoon minced fresh ginger
1/4	cup finely chopped fresh cilantro
1/2	teaspoon salt
1	tablespoon sesame oil
2	teaspoons Sriracha (Thai chile sauce)
1	tablespoon oyster sauce
2	tablespoons sesame seeds, toasted
2	tablespoons cornstarch
2	tablespoons water

16 to 18 spring roll wrappers

Peanut oil, for deep-frying

Mango-Chile Dipping Sauce (page 15)

1. To prepare the filling, in a large bowl, combine the pork, lobster, carrot, won bok, onions, garlic, ginger, and cilantro. Toss and mix well.

2. In a small bowl, combine the salt, sesame oil, Sriracha, oyster sauce, and sesame seeds. Pour this mixture over the filling mixture and mix well.

3. In a small bowl, stir together the cornstarch and water. On a large clean work surface, lay out a spring roll wrapper with a point facing you. Place 2 heaping tablespoons of the filling across the bottom of the wrapper, about 2 inches above the point. Fold the bottom point up over the filling and fold in the sides toward the middle. Put a dab of the cornstarch mixture on the top point. Starting at the bottom, roll up to form a tidy bundle. Repeat with the remaining filling and wrappers. Place the spring rolls on a pan; cover and chill for at least 1 hour before frying.

4. Line a plate with paper towels. In a heavy saucepan, heat about 2 inches of oil to 375 degrees F. Add 2 spring rolls and fry, turning with tongs to fry evenly, for 1 1/2 to 2 minutes, until crisp and browned. Remove the spring rolls from the oil with tongs; drain on the plate. Repeat with the remaining rolls.

5. Serve hot with Mango-Chile Dipping Sauce.

Makes 16 to 18 spring rolls

ingredient notes: *Sriracha sauce is a Thai chile, garlic, and vinegar sauce named for a seaside town in Thailand, and is one among many Asian chile sauces. You'll recognize this one: it comes in a plastic squirt bottle with a bright green cap.*

Spring roll wrappers, fresh or frozen, are made from flour and water in thin squares or rounds, about 6 to 7 inches in diameter. They are different from egg roll wrappers, which contain eggs, and lumpia wrappers, which contain cornstarch.

rack of lamb *with hunan sauce*

This lamb dish has been on the Hali'imaile General Store menu for twenty years, and even if we put another lamb dish on the menu, this one is still the most popular. I cannot tell a lie: I stole this recipe from another book, but tweaked it and put our touches on it.

2	tablespoons white sesame seeds, toasted
5	tablespoons hoisin sauce
3	tablespoons honey
2	tablespoons dark soy sauce
2	tablespoons dry sherry
1	tablespoon sesame oil
1	tablespoon curry powder (any brand)
1	teaspoon sambal oelek (Indonesian chile sauce)
4	garlic cloves, finely minced
1	tablespoon grated orange peel
1	tablespoon salted black beans, rinsed and chopped
2	(8-bone racks) of lamb

1. In a large bowl, combine all the ingredients, except the lamb, and stir well.

2. Cut the lamb into 2-bone chops. Place the lamb in the bowl and marinate in the sauce for 2 hours.

3. Preheat a gas or charcoal grill.

4. Drain the lamb, reserving the marinade in a small saucepan. Over medium-high heat, grill the lamb to desired doneness, about 10 to 12 minutes for medium rare.

5. Bring the marinade to a boil over medium heat. Lower the heat and simmer for a few minutes. Pour the marinade through a fine-mesh strainer into a bowl and serve alongside the lamb.

Serves 4

ingredient note: *Salted black beans are black beans that have been fermented with salt, a pungent ingredient used in Chinese cooking. They should be rinsed and chopped before using. They come in a jar, can, or bag and can be stored in a covered container in the refrigerator for several months. Salted black beans are available in Asian food stores.*

kona coffee-marinated rack of lamb

Kona coffee, one of Hawai'i's best-loved products, flavors the marinade and creates a great crust on tender lamb chops, grilled to perfection. I give you permission to pick up that bone and suck the meat off of it. I like to serve this with the Potato-Plum Casserole (page 106).

8   cups strong, freshly brewed Kona coffee

3   tablespoons dark molasses

2   tablespoons honey

5   star anise, crushed

2   teaspoons whole black peppercorns

1   tablespoon oyster sauce

1   bay leaf

2   teaspoons coriander seeds

2   tablespoons pure vanilla extract

4   (8-bone) racks of lamb, trimmed

1   tablespoon Demi-Glace (page 12)

1   tablespoon butter

Salt

Freshly ground black pepper

1   tablespoon oil

Fresh herb sprigs (such as rosemary or parsley), for garnish

ingredient note: *Oyster sauce is a Chinese bottled product made of oysters and soy sauce. It is thick, dark brown, and has a concentrated flavor. It is used in cooking as well as a condiment, and is available wherever Asian ingredients are sold.*

1. To make the marinade, in a saucepan over medium-high heat, combine the coffee, molasses, honey, star anise, peppercorns, oyster sauce, bay leaf, and coriander seeds. Bring the mixture to a boil, reduce the heat to low, add the vanilla, and simmer for 5 minutes. Cool.

2. To prepare the lamb, place it into a large bowl and cover with 3 cups of the marinade, tossing the racks to coat them well. Cover and refrigerate the chops and marinate for 3 to 4 hours. Remove the lamb from the marinade. Reserve the marinade. Set the lamb aside and allow it to come to room temperature.

3. To make the sauce, in a saucepan over medium-high heat, add the marinade. Bring to a boil, decrease the heat to medium, and reduce to 1 cup, about 20 to 30 minutes. Strain the liquid through a fine-mesh strainer into another saucepan. Place the saucepan over medium heat and bring to a simmer. Whisk in the demi-glace until smooth. Remove from the heat and whisk in the butter. Keep warm until ready to serve.

4. Preheat the oven to 350 degrees F.

5. Season the lamb racks with salt and pepper. In a large ovenproof sauté pan over high heat, add the oil and sear the lamb on all sides until browned and caramelized. Transfer to the oven and roast for 10 to 12 minutes or until a meat thermometer registers 130 degrees F. Remove from the oven and let the lamb rest for 10 minutes before slicing.

6. To serve, slice the lamb into chops and place 4 lamb chops on each plate. Drizzle the sauce around the plate and onto the chops. Garnish with fresh herb sprigs.

Serves 8

braised lamb shanks *with goat cheese grits*

When my father ate several lamb shanks at a sitting, they were not very big. Today we get shanks that are 22 ounces; they're brontosaurus bones! But my customers love braised meats and they're on the menu at Joe's in Wailea every winter.

LAMB SHANKS

8	lamb shanks, approximately 12 ounces each

Salt

Freshly ground black pepper

1	cup flour
1/2	cup olive oil
1	cup diced celery
1	cup peeled and diced carrots
2	cups diced onions
1	tablespoon finely chopped garlic
1	tablespoon finely chopped shallots
8	cups beef or lamb stock
1	cup red wine
1	tablespoon chopped fresh thyme
1	tablespoon chopped fresh rosemary
2	bay leaves
8	fresh thyme sprigs, for garnish
8	fresh rosemary sprigs, for garnish

GOAT CHEESE GRITS

4	cups chicken stock
4	cups whole milk
1	tablespoon salt
2	cups coarse ground cornmeal
1	cup butter
12	ounces goat cheese

1. To prepare the lamb, season the lamb shanks with salt and pepper. Season the flour with salt and pepper. Dredge the shanks in the flour.

2. In a large Dutch oven over high heat, add the olive oil. When the oil is hot, add the shanks in batches, searing until they are browned on all sides. Transfer the shanks to a large plate and set aside.

3. Decrease the heat to medium. Add the celery, carrots, and onions to the pan. Cook for 3 minutes. Add the garlic and shallots and cook for 1 minute. Add 1 cup of the stock to the pan and deglaze, scraping the pan to loosen any browned bits. Add the rest of the stock and the red wine. Bring the liquid to a boil. Add the thyme, rosemary, and bay leaves. Reduce the heat to a simmer and add the lamb shanks to the pot. Cover and cook the lamb shanks until tender, approximately 1 1/2 to 2 hours.

4. When the shanks are cooked, transfer them from the pot to a platter and keep them warm. Strain the sauce through a sieve into another pot. Discard the vegetables. Place the pot over medium-high heat and reduce the sauce until thick. While the sauce reduces, prepare the grits.

5. To make the grits, in a large saucepan over medium-high heat, bring the chicken stock, milk, and salt to a boil. Gradually add the cornmeal to the boiling liquid, continually stirring with a whisk. Decrease the heat to low, cover and cook, stir occasionally to make sure that the grits are not lumping up. Cook for 30 minutes, or until soft and creamy. Stir in the butter and mix well. Add the goat cheese and blend. Keep warm.

6. To serve, place a large spoonful of grits on the bottom of a plate. Place a shank on top. Pour the sauce over the shank. Garnish with thyme and rosemary sprigs.

Serves 8

ingredient note: *Also known as chèvre, goat cheese—fresh, soft, and mild—is my favorite thing to use when I want to add a luscious creaminess to fillings and toppings. I try to use goat cheese produced here in Hawai'i by small producers.*

Chicken, Duck, and Quail

WHEN I WAS GROWING UP, my mother's rotisserie chickens were succulent and juicy, their plump flesh so flavorful and tasty. We got our fill of these delicious birds then looked forward to the casseroles, salads, and sandwiches that Mom would serve in the following days. She was smart, you know, cooking up extra chickens so she'd have leftovers to transform into meals.

There's so much you can do with chicken—whole, breasts, thighs. I love simple whole-roasted chicken, stuffed with garlic and lemons poked with holes to release the juices, browned to a crisp. Or, if I have some truffles around, I like to chop them and mix them with unsalted butter and stuff it under the skin of the chicken. Ooh, it's so delicious.

After enjoying the savory bird, I like to strip the leftover meat for a multitude of preparations ranging from salads to snacks to casseroles to pot pies. And don't forget to save the bones to make the simple chicken stock that forms the base for soups and adds depth to braised dishes and sauces.

Just remember that your choice of chicken makes a big difference. Sadly today's mass-produced poultry are not as flavorful as the chickens I grew up on. If you're used to regular supermarket chicken, you'll be amazed at how much of a difference there is in an organic free-range bird or a kosher chicken, even if they're frozen. I prefer to use these, and if you can find them and afford them, it's worth it. Otherwise you may as well cook paper and put a sauce on it.

Turkey is another favorite of mine. When I first moved to Maui, I'd prepare a turkey dinner once a month; it was my way of giving thanks to living in paradise. I still love turkey dinners—

I even have turkey on the menu for Hawaiian Airlines at Thanksgiving. And if you get a chance to have kālua turkey, cooked in a Hawaiian underground oven lined with hot rocks and banana and ti leaves, you're in for a treat.

With chicken and turkey, it's the dark meat that's my favorite because it's the most flavorful and tender. The satisfying taste of dark meat is well worth the few extra calories it has compared to the breast. Just remember that cooking methods and seasonings can help make chicken deliciously good.

When it comes to duck, I am definitely a fan. It just has more complexity in flavor and texture than chicken or turkey. Most people are afraid to cook it because of all the fat, but it's really simple to release the fat and get a crisp skin. And if you do it right, it is divine. I probably use duck more than any other poultry for parties and special events.

Chicken, turkey, and duck—I love them all! And I can't forget quail, my favorite game bird that has become a signature item on my menus.

Chicken, Duck, and Quail

chicken *with* wild mushrooms, *olives, and artichoke hearts*

The flavors of the Mediterranean are so wonderful to pair with chicken. For the best flavor, splurge on some free-range chicken breasts and find a good assortment of fresh mushrooms. Kalamata, picholine, amphissa, and gaeta are some of the olives I like to use in this dish. You can substitute grape or cherry tomatoes for the yellow teardrop and Sweet 100 varieties but only if they're sweet and flavorful. Long strands of pasta would make a fine accompaniment to this mélange of flavors. If you can manage it, have two sauté pans going at once, just like a chef!

6	(6-ounce) boneless skin-on chicken breasts

Salt

Freshly ground black pepper

6	tablespoons olive oil
2	tablespoons white wine
1¹/₂	pounds assorted fresh mushrooms (shiitake, oyster, lobster, portobello, cremini)
1	cup quartered artichoke hearts, fresh or frozen
5	cloves garlic, finely chopped
1	tablespoon finely chopped shallot
²/₃	cup pitted and halved assorted olives
1	tablespoon capers
3	tablespoons tomato paste
1	cup rich chicken stock
2	tablespoons butter
¹/₂	cup yellow teardrop tomatoes
¹/₂	cup Sweet 100 tomatoes, or other cherry tomatoes
1	tablespoon finely chopped fresh chives
1	tablespoon fresh thyme
2	tablespoon chiffonade of fresh basil, for garnish
3	tablespoons pine nuts, toasted, for garnish

1. To prepare the chicken, season the breasts with salt and pepper. In a large sauté pan over medium-high heat, add 3 tablespoons of the olive oil. When the oil is hot, place the chicken in the pan skin side down. Cook the chicken until the skin is dark golden brown, about 3 to 4 minutes. Turn the chicken over, lower the heat to medium, and cook for 3 to 4 more minutes, or until cooked through. Transfer the chicken to a warm platter and keep warm.

2. Add 2 tablespoons white wine to the pan to deglaze it, scraping any bits from the bottom. Remove the pan from the heat.

3. While the chicken breasts are cooking, heat another large sauté pan over high heat and add the remaining 3 tablespoons of olive oil. Add the mushrooms and sauté for 3 to 4 minutes until lightly browned. Add the artichoke hearts, garlic, and shallot and cook for 2 minutes. Add the olives, capers, and tomato paste and cook for 1 minute. Add the 1 cup of chicken stock and reduce the heat to medium-high; simmer until the liquid is reduced and the mixture thickens. Season with salt and pepper. The mushroom mixture should take the same time to cook as the chicken breasts.

4. Add the deglazed sauce from the chicken pan to the mushroom mixture. Add the butter to the mixture and stir well.

5. Add the tomatoes to the mushroom mixture and gently toss to incorporate. Add the chives and thyme and stir to incorporate. Pour the

ingredient note: *For a chiffonade of basil, stack several basil leaves on top of each other. Roll the leaves up tightly lengthwise, then cut the roll into very fine slices.*

mushroom mixture over the chicken breasts. Garnish with the basil and pine nuts. Serve immediately.

Serves 6

buttermilk fried chicken

As a kid growing up in Texas, fried chicken was a staple in our house. We got it from Youngblood's down the street, where double-battered fried chicken drizzled with honey had no equal. At various times when I was growing up, my mother was fortunate enough to have help in the kitchen. Lula Mae was one of our favorite "mother's helpers," and she made the best fried chicken ever. I know it had a lot to do with the overnight buttermilk marinade and good old Lawry's salts.

2	tablespoons salt
2	tablespoons Lawry's lemon pepper
2	tablespoons garlic powder
3	pounds bone-in chicken pieces, breasts and thighs
2	cups buttermilk
3	cups flour
3	tablespoons Lawry's seasoned salt
2	cups vegetable shortening, preferably Crisco

1. In a small mixing bowl, mix together the salt and 1 tablespoon each of the lemon pepper and garlic powder. Season the chicken pieces with the salt mixture. Place the chicken in a baking pan, one layer deep. Pour in the buttermilk. Cover and marinate the chicken overnight in the refrigerator.

2. When you're ready to cook the chicken, remove it from the refrigerator and bring it to room temperature. Mix together the flour, seasoned salt, and the remaining 1 tablespoon each of lemon pepper and garlic powder in a large paper bag.

3. In a large cast iron skillet over medium-high heat, melt the shortening and heat to 375 degrees F.

4. Drain the chicken well. Add the chicken, a few pieces at a time, to the flour in the bag and shake to coat. Fill the skillet with coated chicken pieces, skin-side down. Fry the chicken until the skin is golden brown, about 8 to 10 minutes. Turn the chicken pieces over and fry another 8 to 10 minutes until the chicken is cooked through. Transfer the cooked chicken to a platter and keep warm. Bring the oil temperature back to 375 degrees F and cook the rest of the chicken pieces.

5. Serve immediately.

Serves 6

coconut chicken skewers

We do a lot of chef events—walk-around, grazing affairs where chefs do a couple of appetizer-size dishes, usually fancy ones with ten steps. With this quintessential *pūpū* (appetizer), my line is usually longer than anyone else's. I have made thousands and thousands of these; everyone loves them. You can make them ahead: freeze them between layers of parchment paper then store them in a plastic bag in the freezer.

2	pounds boneless, skinless chicken breasts
2	cups shredded sweetened coconut
2	cups shredded unsweetened coconut
2	cups panko (Japanese breadcrumbs)
1/2	cup sesame seeds, toasted
1	teaspoon salt
1/2	teaspoon freshly ground black pepper
2	cups flour
6	eggs, beaten

Canola or coconut oil, for frying

Mango-Chile Dipping Sauce (page 15)

1. Cut chicken breast into long thin strips and thread the strips onto bamboo skewers.

2. To make the coconut breading mixture, in a shallow bowl mix the sweetened and unsweetened coconut, panko, sesame seeds, salt, and pepper.

3. Dip the chicken skewers in flour then dip into the egg, coating well. Cover with the coconut breading mixture. Set the skewers aside on a tray until all of them are coated. At this point, you can refrigerate the skewers until you are ready to fry or freeze them.

4. To cook the chicken, use a deep skillet or deep fryer. Heat 3 to 4 inches of oil to 375 degrees F. Fry the skewers, a few at a time, until golden brown and crisp, about 3 to 4 minutes. Remove from the oil and drain on paper towels. Serve warm with Mango-Chile Dipping Sauce.

Serves 6

ingredient note: *To toast sesame seeds, place them in an ungreased, small frying pan over medium heat. Toast for 3 to 4 minutes, tossing and stirring, until golden brown. Sesame seeds will burn in a flash, so keep your eye on them.*

mom's chicken and buttermilk dumplings

Chicken and dumplings was my mother's absolute favorite thing to eat. As my mom got on in years, I'd find cans and cans of Sally Bee's chicken and dumplings in her cupboard so she could eat it on a whim. Chicken and dumplings is a dish I remember eating as a child, a Southern comfort food dish that I loved. As kids, the dumplings were the first to be picked out, soft and light with a tangy flavor. The key is to make the dumplings with buttermilk.

CHICKEN

2	tablespoons butter
1/2	cup coarsely chopped onion
1/2	cup chopped celery, including some leaves
1/2	cup peeled and coarsely chopped carrots
3	cloves garlic, crushed
1	(4-pound) whole chicken, preferably organic and free range
10	cups chicken stock

5 or 6 fresh thyme sprigs

Salt

Freshly ground black pepper

2	tablespoons chopped fresh parsley, for garnish
2	teaspoons fresh thyme leaves, for garnish

DUMPLINGS

2	cups flour
1/2	teaspoon salt
2	teaspoons baking powder
2	teaspoons baking soda
2	tablespoons very cold butter, cut into small pieces
1/2	cup buttermilk

1. To prepare the chicken, in a stockpot over medium-high heat, melt the butter. Add the onion, celery, and carrots and cook for two minutes. Add the garlic; cook for one minute. Place the chicken on top of the vegetables and pour in the stock to cover. Bring the stock to a boil and then reduce the heat to a simmer. Add the thyme sprigs. Simmer for one hour, or until the chicken is tender.

2. Remove the chicken from the stock and set it aside to cool. Strain the stock through a strainer into a saucepan.

3. When the chicken is cool, remove the bones and skin, and cut the meat into large bite-size pieces. Set aside.

4. To prepare the dumplings, place the flour, salt, baking powder, and baking soda in a food processor. Add the butter. Pulse to incorporate the butter into the flour. Through the feed tube, add the buttermilk in a slow stream. When the dough forms a ball, turn off the machine.

5. On a work surface lightly sprinkled with flour, roll the dough out to 2-inch round pieces. Cut the dough into 2-inch square pieces.

6. Bring the chicken stock to a boil then lower the heat to a simmer. Season with salt and pepper. Add the dumplings and gently stir as needed to keep them separated. Cook the dumplings for 4 to 5 minutes or until set. Add the chicken pieces and simmer another 5 minutes while the dumplings thicken the stock. To serve, ladle the chicken and dumplings into bowls and sprinkle with parsley and thyme.

Serves 6

leftovers? Make Chicken, Sausage, and Shiitake Mushroom Pot Pie (page 90)

lemon-rosemary chicken breast
over wild rice pancake

Chicken breasts can be very mild in flavor, so I like to add a lot of zest to them. Marinating them in a flavorful mix of herbs can take them over the top. The most important thing is to not overcook the chicken; practice will make perfect.

CHICKEN

1/3	cup fresh Meyer lemon juice
1	tablespoon minced garlic
1	tablespoon finely chopped fresh rosemary
2	teaspoons finely chopped fresh thyme
1	tablespoon rinsed and chopped preserved lemon (see Ingredient Notes, opposite page)
2	teaspoons cracked black pepper
1	cup olive oil
6	(8-ounce) chicken breasts, boneless

WILD RICE PANCAKE

2	cups wild rice
1	teaspoon salt
2	cloves garlic, minced
6	tablespoons flour
1/2	teaspoon baking powder
2	eggs, lightly beaten
1/2	cup milk, at room temperature
2	tablespoons butter, melted

1. To marinate the chicken, mix together the lemon juice, garlic, rosemary, thyme, preserved lemon, and pepper in a mixing bowl. Slowly whisk in the olive oil and blend well. In a glass dish, place the chicken breasts skin side down and pour the marinade over the chicken. Cover and refrigerate for 4 hours, turning once. If you want to marinate the chicken overnight, mix the marinade without the lemon juice. The next day, 4 hours before cooking the chicken, remove the chicken from the dish and add the lemon juice to the marinade, mixing well to incorporate. Return the chicken to the dish to continue marinating.

2. To make the pancakes, wash the rice by placing it in a bowl and cover with water. Let stand for 5 minutes. Drain the rice through a colander. Place the colander in the sink and run water over the rice for a couple of minutes to further clean.

3. In a 3-quart saucepan filled with water, pour in the rice. Bring the rice to a boil, reduce the heat to a simmer and cook for about 45 to 55 minutes, or until the rice kernels open. Remove the saucepan from the heat and drain the rice through a colander.

4. In a food processor, add the rice, salt, garlic, flour, baking powder, eggs, milk, and melted butter. Pulse to blend. Transfer to a mixing bowl.

5. In a large sauté pan over medium-high heat, add enough butter to coat the pan. By the 1/4 cupful, take the rice mixture and form into round pancakes. Cook the pancakes for 2 minutes, turn the heat down to medium, flip the pancakes, and cook another 3 minutes. Transfer pancakes to a platter and keep warm.

LEMON VINAIGRETTE

3	tablespoons freshly squeezed Meyer lemon juice
1	tablespoon champagne vinegar
2	tablespoons Dijon-style mustard
1	teaspoon chopped fresh chives
1	tablespoon finely diced shallot
1	teaspoon lemon zest
1	teaspoon fresh thyme leaves
1	cup extra virgin olive oil

Salt

Freshly ground black pepper

6. To make the vinaigrette, in a blender, add the lemon juice, vinegar, mustard, chives, shallot, lemon zest, and thyme. Blend until well incorporated. Add the olive oil in a slow steady stream. When the mixture is well blended, season with salt and pepper.

7. When you are ready to cook the chicken, remove the chicken from the marinade. In a large skillet over medium-high heat, sauté the chicken, skin side down for 4 minutes, or until the skin is golden brown. Turn the breasts, lower the heat to medium, and continue cooking for 4 more minutes. While the chicken is cooking, in a small saucepan over low heat, heat the vinaigrette. Do not boil.

8. To serve, place a wild rice pancake in the center of each plate. Place the chicken breast on top. Ladle a spoonful of vinaigrette over the chicken and serve.

Serves 6

ingredient notes: *Meyer lemons are my choice for this recipe because of their flavor. If you taste different lemons side by side, you'll notice there's less of a pucker factor in a Meyer lemon. Use a regular lemon if you can't find a Meyer; just make sure it's a fresh lemon.*

Preserved lemons are a Moroccan preparation of lemons, salted and preserved in lemon juice. To make them, split several whole lemons lengthwise into quarters but do not cut all the way through. Sprinkle the lemons generously with kosher salt and place in a jar. Fill the jar with lemon juice. Cover and refrigerate for at least 2 weeks before using.

roast chicken *with goat cheese*

You could just roast a whole chicken without the goat cheese under the skin. But having something between the skin and meat adds a whole other dimension to a roast chicken. I love to use truffles, foie gras, and mushroom duxelles under the skin; lots of herb butter works for me too. One thing to remember: let this chicken rest for 10 to 15 minutes before you cut into it, otherwise the cheese will melt out of it.

1   (4 to 5-pound) chicken, fryer or broiler

Salt

Freshly ground black pepper

8 to 10 stems fresh tarragon

1   lemon, quartered

$1/2$ cup butter, at room temperature

3   ounces soft goat cheese, at room temperature

$1/4$ cup coarsely chopped onions

$1/4$ cup peeled and coarsely chopped carrots

$1/4$ cup white wine

$3/4$ cup rich chicken stock

1. Preheat the oven to 425 degrees F.

2. To prepare the chicken, rinse the chicken under cool water, inside and out. Remove any fat from inside the cavity and from the neck area of the chicken. Pat the chicken completely dry with paper towels. Fold the wings back and under the breast. Carefully separate the skin from the meat at the breast.

3. Generously season the cavity of the chicken with salt and pepper. Stuff the cavity with the tarragon and quartered lemon.

4. In a small bowl, cream together $1/4$ cup of the butter and the goat cheese. Using your hands, mold this mixture into 2 flattened patties that are the size of each breast. Place each patty between the skin and the breast, flatten the cheese out and spread it over the entire breast area.

5. Spread the remaining $1/4$ cup of butter over the entire chicken. Season the chicken generously with salt.

6. With a piece of kitchen twine, tie the drumsticks together. Place the chicken, breast side up, in a shallow roasting pan fitted with an oiled v-shaped roasting rack.

7. Place the pan into the oven. After 15 minutes, decrease the heat to 350 degrees F. After 30 minutes, add the onions and carrots to the pan. Continue to roast the chicken for 45 to 60 minutes. To check for doneness, pierce the thigh; the juices should run clear with no pink. Or insert an instant-read thermometer into the thigh meat; it should register 165 degrees F. When the chicken is cooked, remove it from the oven and transfer it to a platter to rest for 10 to 15 minutes before carving.

8. To make the sauce, remove the rack from the pan. Place the pan over a burner over medium heat. When the pan juices are hot, add the white

continued on page 148

wine and deglaze the pan, scraping bits off the bottom of the pan with a spatula. Add the chicken stock and cook for 4 minutes, stirring constantly until the sauce has reduced a little. Strain the sauce through a fine-mesh strainer into a bowl and serve alongside the chicken.

Serves 6

leftovers? I always roast a couple of chickens at a time, with or without the goat cheese stuffing. Use plain roast chicken to make Chicken and Caramelized Onion Crêpes with Mixed Mushroom Sauce (page 32) or Barbecued Chicken and Smoked Gouda Quesadilla (page 149). Leftover chicken can top a salad, be the protein in a stir-fry of vegetables and pasta, star in sandwiches and chicken tacos, and add substance to a simple chicken and vegetable soup. There's so much you can do with leftover chicken that it's worth it to roast a couple once a week.

barbecued chicken and smoked gouda quesadilla

I'm always looking for menu items that people can share at the table, just like you would at home. This quesadilla is served at Joe's in Wailea; it's easy to pick up and eat, perfect for a table of four. It's the ultimate Texas barbecue in a crunchy tortilla and the perfect reflection of how I cook with simple ingredients.

CHICKEN QUESADILLA FILLING

2   teaspoons ground cumin

1   teaspoon garlic powder

2   teaspoons chipotle chile powder

1   tablespoon salt

2   teaspoons finely ground black pepper

1   pound chicken breast or thighs, boneless and skinless

3   tablespoons oil

3/4 cup Hali'imaile Barbecue Sauce (page 14)

1/2 cup finely diced fresh pineapple

1   tablespoon light brown sugar

12 (6-inch) flour tortillas

2   tablespoons chopped fresh cilantro

1   pound smoked Gouda, shredded

CHIPOTLE SOUR CREAM

1   cup sour cream

1   tablespoon freshly squeezed lime juice

2   tablespoons mashed chipotle chile in adobo sauce

1. To prepare the chicken, in a small bowl, mix together the cumin, garlic powder, chile powder, salt, and pepper. Place the chicken on a plate and rub the spice mixture all over the chicken pieces.

2. In a large sauté pan over medium heat, add 1 tablespoon of the oil. Add the chicken and cook for 3 minutes. Turn and cook the chicken for another 3 to 4 minutes, or until the chicken is cooked through. Transfer the chicken to a plate to cool. When the chicken is cool, cut the chicken into julienne strips and place in a bowl. Add the barbecue sauce and toss. Set aside.

3. In a small nonstick sauté pan over medium-high heat, place the pineapple. Sprinkle the brown sugar over the pineapple and cook, stirring occasionally, until the pineapple caramelizes. Transfer the pineapple to the bowl of chicken and mix well.

4. On a flat surface, lay out 6 tortillas. Divide the chicken among the tortillas. Sprinkle the cilantro over the chicken then divide the cheese evenly over the chicken. Place another tortilla on top of each portion, and press down to flatten the mixture. Brush both sides of the tortilla with the remaining 2 tablespoons of oil.

5. To make the chipotle cream, in a small bowl, mix together the sour cream, lime juice, and chipotle chile until well blended. Set aside.

6. In a large nonstick pan over medium-high heat, place a filled tortilla in the pan, pressing down with a spatula. Cook until golden brown and crisp. Flip the tortilla and cook the other side until golden brown. Repeat until all the filled tortillas are cooked. Transfer to a plate, cut into quarters, and serve with the chipotle cream.

Serves 6

seared duck breast
with corn fritters and maple sauce

Duck is my favorite poultry and searing a duck breast is as simple as searing a chicken breast. But it's the corn fritters that will make you shout, "Wow!" When I put my creative hat on for a charity dinner I was doing for long-time customers, I could have skipped the duck and maple sauce and just made these corn fritters! If I can make fritters this good, so can you!

DUCK

6	(8-ounce) duck breasts

Salt

Freshly ground black pepper

2	cups rich chicken stock
1/3	cup pure maple syrup
1	teaspoon olive oil

CORN FRITTERS

1	cup flour
1	teaspoon baking powder
1/2	teaspoon salt
1/4	teaspoon sugar
1	egg
1	(14-ounce) can creamed corn
1	tablespoon butter, melted
1	cup fresh corn kernels

Corn oil, for frying

1. To prepare the duck, on a cutting board, using a sharp knife, score the skin of the duck breasts by making 3 to 4 cuts in one direction across the breast, then making 3 to 4 cuts in the opposite direction to form a diamond pattern on the skin. Season both sides of the duck with salt and pepper and set aside.

2. In a saucepan, over medium-high heat, bring the chicken stock to a boil until reduced to 1 cup. Add the maple syrup and heat through. Set aside and keep warm.

3. To make the fritters, in a bowl, sift together the flour, baking powder, salt, and sugar. In another bowl, crack the egg and beat lightly with a whisk. Add the creamed corn and the melted butter to the egg and blend together. Add the corn mixture to the flour mixture and mix. Stir in the fresh corn kernels.

4. In a heavy saucepan, over high heat, heat 3 to 4 inches of corn oil to 350 degrees F. Using a 1/4-cup scoop, drop the batter into the hot oil and fry until golden brown. Remove from the oil and drain on paper towels. Continue to fry the fritters until all the batter is used.

5. In a large sauté pan over medium-high heat, add the olive oil. Place the duck, skin side down, in the pan and cook until the skin is browned and the fat is rendered, about 6 to 8 minutes. Turn the breast over and reduce the heat to low and cook the duck for another 5 to 6 minutes for medium rare. Transfer the duck to a platter and let it rest for 5 to 6 minutes.

6. Slice each duck breast into 6 pieces on the diagonal and fan the slices onto a dinner plate. Drizzle the sauce around the duck; serve a few fritters alongside.

Serves 6

apricot and pistachio-stuffed quail

Any cookbook of mine has to have a recipe for quail. It's my favorite thing to eat, especially when it's prepared with fruits and nuts, a nice balance of flavor for game birds. I like to stuff quail so they're plump and pretty on the plate. I can't think of anything better!

APRICOT AND PISTACHIO STUFFING

6	strips thick smoked bacon, cut into 1/4-inch pieces
2	tablespoons finely minced shallots
8	tablespoons butter
1/2	pound cremini mushrooms, finely diced
1/4	cup finely diced celery
1/2	pound Black Forest ham, finely diced
1/2	cup finely diced dried apricots
1/4	cup toasted and coarsely chopped pistachios
1	cup crumbled cornbread
1/4	cup chicken stock
1	large egg, beaten
12	semiboneless quail

Salt

Freshly ground black pepper

SAUCE

2	cups Demi-Glace (page 12)
1/2	cup port wine

1. To prepare the stuffing, in a large sauté pan over medium heat, add the bacon and cook until bacon is just turning crisp, about 4 minutes. Add the shallots and sauté for 30 seconds, stirring. Increase the heat to medium high and melt 2 tablespoons of the butter. Add the mushrooms and cook for 1 minute. Add the celery, ham, and apricots and cook for 1 minute. Add the pistachios and cook for 1 minute, stirring constantly. Remove from the heat and add the cornbread. Add the chicken stock and mix together. Set aside to cool. When the mixture is cool, add the egg and mix well.

2. Preheat the oven to 400 degrees F.

3. Stuff the cavity of each quail with the stuffing mixture. Using a toothpick, close the cavity of the quail. With some string, tie the legs together, forming a neat, plump bird. Rub the quail with the remaining 6 tablespoons of butter and season with salt and pepper. Place the quail in a roasting pan and into the oven. Roast for 5 minutes. Decrease the heat to 350 degrees F and roast for 25 minutes, or until the quail are cooked through.

4. To make the sauce, while the quail is roasting, place the demi-glace in a 1-quart saucepan over medium-high heat, and bring to a boil. Decrease the heat, and reduce the liquid by one-third. Add the wine, decrease the heat to medium low, and simmer for 10 to 12 minutes, or until the sauce thickens.

5. To serve, ladle the sauce on a plate and place two quail per person on top of the sauce.

Serves 6

Soups and Salads

HONESTLY, IT WASN'T UNTIL the last ten years or so that I liked soup. I never ordered soup, I was never a fan of soup, and I never understood why people ate so much soup!

Perhaps it was because soup in our house was a can of Campbell's or a package of Lipton's. My mother did, though, make a great chicken soup with matzo balls or kreplach (filled dumplings). Her goal in life was to make fluffy, light matzo balls, just like my Jewish aunts did when they came to Dallas a few times a year. She never got it.

When I opened Hali'imaile General Store, a chef named David (we called him Gracie when he made soup) taught me to make great soups. When he left, I took over and now I see why people order soups.

Soups are comfort food, a warm meal in a bowl or a taste of something to whet your appetite for the next course. They can be light and luxurious like cold beet borscht or hearty and filling like a good chicken soup that's all about lots of vegetables and chicken. I don't like to put rice or noodles in soup; I do like to add flavors like ginger, lemongrass, and other fresh herbs.

Of course, the basis of good soup is a good stock—beef, veal, chicken, fish, seafood, or vegetable. Take the time to make a batch and freeze it if need be so you always have homemade stock on hand. Good stock means good soup.

Salads were not very creative in my house either. Romaine or head lettuce was the salad, served with bottled dressings—six of them on the dining table so everyone had their favorite. My favorite dressing has always been blue cheese.

Today my favorite way to dress a salad is a drizzle of good olive, pumpkin, or walnut oil, followed by a drizzle of one-hundred-year-old balsamic vinegar. While the latter is not always possible, I use a champagne vinegar or a fruit vinegar like fig or raspberry. The important thing is to drizzle and toss, drizzle and toss, so that each flavor is layered on the greens along with herbs and seasonings. The layers of flavor combine when you eat it all together—this is salad bliss!

It's important to have really fresh greens and ingredients for salad making. Grow your own, or buy greens directly from a farm if you can or at your nearest farmers' market. Locally grown greens will always be fresher and last longer in your refrigerator. Experiment with different greens, soft or crunchy, mild or spicy, green or red. They can all be combined in one bowl, topped with proteins, cheeses, nuts, herbs, or whatever is at hand. Creating entrée salads that are different and delicious is fun for me. It will be for you too, if you just get into the kitchen and do it!

Soups and Salads

butternut squash soup
with coconut and ginger

I don't know when I became a fan of butternut squash, but I think it's the best-tasting of winter squashes. It's sweet and flavorful on its own, it's easy to cook, and it's good for you. The coconut and ginger give this soup an Asian twist; I've made this on the *Today Show*.

1   **(5-pound) butternut squash**

6   **tablespoons butter, at room temperature**

Salt

Freshly ground black pepper

1   **medium onion, finely chopped**

2   **shallots, finely chopped**

3   **tablespoons finely minced fresh ginger**

1   **cup unsweetened coconut milk**

6   **cups vegetable stock**

Toasted coconut, for garnish

1. Preheat the oven to 350 degrees F.

2. To prepare the squash, cut it in half lengthwise. Remove the seeds. On a baking sheet, place the squash, cut side up. Rub the inside of each squash half with 1 tablespoon of butter and season with salt and pepper. Roast the squash, uncovered, for about 1 hour or until tender. Remove from the oven, cool , and scoop the cooked flesh into a bowl.

3. In a large saucepan over medium-high heat, melt the remaining 4 tablespoons of butter. Add the onion, shallots, and ginger and cook for about 5 minutes, or until the onions are wilted. Add the cooked squash, coconut milk, and vegetable stock. Reduce the heat to low and simmer for 20 minutes.

4. Using an immersion blender, purée the soup until smooth. Or, in small batches, add the squash mixture to a blender and blend until smooth. Season with salt and pepper. Ladle into soup bowls and garnish with toasted coconut.

Serves 6

ingredient notes: *You're lucky if you live Hawai'i when it comes to ginger: it's grown here and we get the best and freshest of the crop. When you're using fresh ginger, be sure to peel it; use a paring knife or vegetable peeler or simply scrape the light brown skin off with a spoon. Look for mature ginger with smooth skin; shriveled skin indicates older ginger. The older ginger is, the more stringy it is.*

To make toasted coconut, place shredded coconut on a baking pan and place in 300-degree-F oven for about 5 minutes or until golden brown.

cauliflower soup

Cauliflower is one of my favorite vegetables. It's one of those vegetables that doesn't get the play it needs—you don't often see it on restaurant menus. One night I was having some people over for dinner, and I had a craving for cauliflower and soup. So I created this soup and have been eating it ever since. Be sure your cauliflower is fresh and without any blemishes.

2   tablespoons butter

1/2   cup chopped onions

2   tablespoons peeled and chopped carrot

2   shallots, chopped

3   pounds cauliflower, broken into florets

8   cups chicken stock

1   cup heavy cream, at room temperature

Salt

Freshly ground white pepper

1   tablespoon truffle oil, for garnish

1   tablespoon Chive Oil, for garnish (page 14)

1. In a 6-quart saucepan over medium heat, melt the butter. Add the onions, carrots, and shallots, and sauté for 2 minutes. Add the cauliflower and the chicken stock. Bring to a boil, reduce the heat, and simmer for 45 minutes, or until the cauliflower is tender.

2. With a slotted spoon or strainer, transfer the cauliflower to a bowl. Strain the broth through a fine-mesh sieve into a bowl; discard the other vegetables. In a blender, purée the cauliflower in batches, adding the strained stock as needed to create a smooth consistency. Transfer the puréed cauliflower and any remaining stock to a clean saucepan. Over low heat, add the cream, whisking to blend well and heat until warm. Season with salt and pepper. Ladle the soup into bowls and garnish with a drizzle of truffle oil and Chive Oil.

Serves 6

leftovers? Serve it with scallops. Reduce the soup over medium-low heat until it is really thick. Sear a fresh scallop and place it on top of a portion of the thickened soup, drizzle with truffle and chive oil. You'll be amazed at how well the two flavors marry!

lemongrass gazpacho *with chile crab*

I love cold soups, but there aren't too many around. Gazpacho is one of my favorites, and I've added some Asian flavors and chile crab to spice this one up. This is a great lunch dish to take to the beach. It's healthy too.

LEMONGRASS GAZPACHO

1	large onion, quartered
3	ribs celery, coarsely chopped
1	cucumber, peeled and seeded, coarsely chopped
4	tomatoes, quartered
2	cups loosely packed fresh cilantro leaves
1	tablespoon finely chopped lemongrass
4	teaspoons freshly squeezed lime juice
2	teaspoons freshly squeezed lemon juice

Salt

2	teaspoons sambal oelek (Indonesian chile sauce)
1	teaspoon freshly ground black pepper
5	cups tomato juice
6	shiso (perilla) leaves, finely julienned, for garnish

CHILE CRAB

1	pound blue crab, or lump crabmeat
2	tablespoons mayonnaise
2	teaspoons sambal oelek (Indonesian chile sauce)
2	teaspoons sesame seeds, toasted
2	teaspoons freshly squeezed lemon juice

1. To prepare the gazpacho, place the onions and the celery in a food processor and pulse to chop. Add the cucumber and pulse again. Add the remaining ingredients except the tomato juice and shiso, and pulse until all the ingredients are finely chopped but well mixed. Add the tomato juice and pulse once or twice. Transfer to a bowl, cover, and refrigerate until well chilled.

2. To prepare the crab, combine all the ingredients in a bowl and mix well. Chill until ready to serve.

3. To serve, ladle the gazpacho into a shallow bowl and top with a scoop of the crab. Garnish with shiso and serve.

Serves 6

ingredient notes: *Lemongrass: I love the herbal flavor of this tropical grass. It can be found fresh in Southeast Asian markets and it is also available dried and shredded. Lemongrass freezes well too. Use only the bottom 6 inches of a lemongrass stalk and remove the fibrous outer leaves. To chop it, use a knife for best results; crush the stalk if you're using it whole to release its aromatic essence.*

Shiso, which is related to mint, is the leaf of the perilla or beefsteak plant. It is often used with raw fish in sushi bars, and it's best eaten raw and fresh because it loses its flavor when cooked. Find it at Japanese markets or farmers' markets

corn and crab chowder

I've been on a quest for the best corn chowder for years and this is it. For me, chowder has to be more about the chunkiness of it rather than the soupiness. It has to have a lot of corn and, in this case, lots of crab—flavors that you taste with every bite you take. Otherwise don't tell me it's a corn and crab chowder.

6	slices applewood-smoked bacon, cut into 1/2-inch pieces
2	tablespoons butter
1/4	cup finely chopped celery
1/4	cup finely chopped onions
3	cloves garlic, finely minced
1	cup fresh corn kernels
1 1/2	pounds crabmeat
5	cups fish stock (page 11), or clam juice
2	cups 1-inch cubes peeled Yukon gold potatoes
1	cup heavy cream
2	tablespoons chopped fresh parsley
1	tablespoon fresh thyme leaves

Salt

Freshly ground white pepper

1. In a 4-quart stockpot over medium-high heat, add the bacon and cook until the bacon is crispy. Add the butter and when it has melted, add the celery, onions, and garlic and sauté for 2 minutes. Add the corn and sauté for 2 minutes. Add 1 pound of the crab, the fish stock, and the potatoes. Bring to a boil and then reduce to a simmer. Simmer for 30 to 40 minutes or until the potatoes are cooked. Add the cream, parsley, and thyme. Season with salt and pepper. When the chowder is thoroughly heated, ladle into bowls. Garnish with the remaining 1/2 pound of crab and serve.

Serves 6

ingredient note: *Hawai'i grows some of the sweetest corn on earth. I love to pick up a fresh ear and just chomp on the sweet kernels without even cooking it. To get fresh kernels off the cob, simply cut them off with a knife. Try do to it on a cutting board in your sink: the kernels are guaranteed to fly everywhere!*

russian beet borscht

When I think of borscht, I see my father's four sisters standing in the kitchen, picking on each other and yelling at each other: "Too much meat," "Put this in," "No, put that in!" They always came for holidays and the constant back-and-forth banter made me wonder if anything would turn out right. In the end, the borscht always turned out exactly the same and it was always really good.

4	large red beets
1¹/₂	cups distilled white vinegar
3	pounds stew meat, cut into ¹/₂-inch cubes
8	cups beef stock
2	cups canned chopped tomatoes
¹/₄	cup finely diced celery
¹/₄	cup peeled and finely diced carrots
¹/₄	cup chopped onion
2	cups thinly sliced cabbage
2	teaspoons dried dill
2	bay leaves
1	cup sour cream, for garnish
2	tablespoons chopped fresh dill, for garnish

1. Place the beets in a saucepan and add 1 cup of the vinegar. Add water to cover the beets. Bring to a boil over medium-high heat, cover, and reduce the heat to medium. Cook the beets until tender. When the beets are cooked, remove the beets with a slotted spoon and place them in a bowl to cool.

2. When the beets are cool, shred the beets using a mandoline or a coarse grater. Save the runoff juice; return the shredded beets and juice to the bowl and set aside.

3. Place the beef and the beef stock in a large soup pot. Bring to a boil over medium-high heat, skimming any foam that may rise to the top. Reduce the heat to low and simmer for 1 hour, covered, skimming as needed. Add the tomatoes, celery, carrots, onion, cabbage, dill, bay leaves, and remaining ¹/₂ cup vinegar. Simmer for 1 hour. Add the shredded beets and beet juice. Heat for 5 minutes, or until heated through. Serve with a dollop of sour cream and sprinkle with fresh dill.

Serves 8

white bean and smoked turkey soup

There's nothing better for a Saturday night family supper than a big bowl of hearty soup, crusty bread, and a salad. And a good heartwarming, stick-to-your-bones soup should have beans—I love all kinds of different beans. You could use canned beans in this recipe, but there's something soothing about the process of cooking dried beans that I love.

WHITE BEANS

2	pounds small dried white beans, rinsed and picked over for stones
3	carrots, peeled and cut into 3 pieces each
3	stalks celery, cut in half
1	medium onion, cut in half
3	cloves whole garlic
10	cups chicken stock

SMOKED TURKEY

$^1/_4$	pound natural smoked bacon, cut into $^1/_2$-inch pieces
2	teaspoons finely chopped garlic
2	tablespoons finely chopped shallots
$^1/_4$	cup peeled and finely chopped carrots
$^1/_4$	cup finely chopped celery
$^1/_4$	cup finely chopped leeks, white part only
2	cups julienned smoked turkey
1	tablespoon fresh thyme leaves
1	tablespoon fresh oregano leaves
2	tablespoons chopped fresh parsley, for garnish

1. In a large stockpot over high heat, place the beans, carrots, celery, onion, garlic, and chicken stock. Cover the pot and bring to a boil over high heat. Reduce the heat to a simmer. Cook the beans for about 2 hours or until the beans are just tender, occasionally skimming off any foam that may rise to the top. Add more stock or water if needed.

2. When the beans are cooked, remove the vegetables and garlic from the beans and discard. Using a fine-mesh sieve, strain the liquid into a large bowl, keeping the strainer with the beans over the bowl.

3. In the same stockpot over medium-high heat, add the bacon and cook until the bacon begins to brown. Add the garlic, shallots, carrots, celery, and leeks and cook for 3 minutes. Add the turkey. Add the beans. Add enough of the reserved stock to just cover the ingredients in the pot. Lower the heat to a simmer and cook for 30 minutes. Add the thyme and oregano. Cook for 10 minutes more and serve, garnished with parsley.

Serves 8 to 10

leftovers? White beans can be used in the Grilled Chicken Panzanella Salad (page 169). Or serve them with a good-quality canned oil-packed tuna. White beans are also terrific alongside a leg of lamb, roast chicken, or just about anything.

warm goat cheese tart
with curried crab and microgreens

There's not a better appetizer-salad combination than this: a savory crust (in place of bread), a creamy cheesy filling, and microgreens to top it off. Goat cheese is one of my favorite cheeses to cook with, and I always have it in some combination on my menu.

GOAT CHEESE TART

- 16 ounces cream cheese, at room temperature
- 8 ounces fresh goat cheese, at room temperature
- 4 eggs
- 1/2 cup heavy cream
- 2 teaspoons ground nutmeg
- 2 tablespoons chopped fresh chives
- 1 teaspoon salt
- 1/2 teaspoon freshly ground black pepper
- 8 prebaked 4-inch tart shells
- 1 cup microgreens, for garnish

CURRIED CRAB

- 1 tablespoon yellow curry powder
- 1/2 cup mayonnaise
- 1 teaspoon oil
- 1 pound blue crab meat
- 1 tablespoon minced celery
- 1 tablespoon dried mango, finely diced
- 1 tablespoon diced macadamia nuts

Salt

Freshly ground black pepper

1. Preheat the oven to 350 degrees F.

2. To prepare the tarts, combine the cream cheese and goat cheese.in a food processor and pulse until smooth. Add the eggs, one at a time, pulsing after each addition. Add the cream, nutmeg, chives, salt, and pepper and pulse to blend. Pour the cheese mixture into the tart shells, filling them to the top. Bake for about 25 minutes, or until set in the center. Remove from the oven and cool.

3. To prepare the curried crab, heat a small sauté pan over medium heat. Add the curry powder and toast until fragrant. Remove from the heat and place in a small bowl. Add the mayonnaise and mix well. In a bowl, add the crab, celery, mango, and nuts and gently mix together. Add the curry mayonnaise and combine. Season with salt and pepper.

4. To serve, top each tart with about 1/3 cup of curried crab and a handful of greens.

Serves 4

> **ingredient note:** *Microgreens are tiny, days-old sprouts of lettuces and herbs, barely an inch high. They pack a lot of flavor and add sparkle to a plate. Look for them at farmers' markets or specialty food stores.*

corn, edamame, and jicama slaw

Growing up in Texas, Mexican food was everywhere. Once I fell in love with it, I loved—and still love—to cook it. I love each element in this dish—the jicama, mint, sweet corn, and edamame, and together they're terrific. In the summer when corn is the sweetest, it can be rubbed with the olive oil and cooked on the grill, cooled, and then taken off the cob. Add the lime juice to the bowl of warm corn kernels and then cool.

2	ears fresh corn
1	tablespoon olive oil
1/2	cup cooked and shelled edamame (green soybeans)
2	tablespoons, plus 2 teaspoons freshly squeezed lime juice
1/2	cup mayonnaise
1/2	cup sour cream
1	tablespoon ground cumin

Zest of 1 lime

2	pounds jicama, peeled and julienned to a medium width
2	cups thinly shredded Chinese cabbage
1	tablespoon coarsely chopped fresh cilantro
2	tablespoons coarsely chopped fresh mint

Salt

Freshly ground white pepper

Mint sprigs, for garnish

1. With a knife, remove the corn kernels from the cob; you should have 1 cup of corn kernels.

2. In a sauté pan over high heat, add the olive oil and heat for 1 minute. Add the corn kernels and sauté for one minute. Add the edamame and sauté for one minute. Add one tablespoon of the lime juice, stir, and remove from the heat. Transfer the corn and edamame into a strainer over a bowl and set aside to drain and cool.

3. In a mixing bowl, whisk together the mayonnaise, sour cream, cumin, lime zest, and the remaining 1 tablespoon plus 2 teaspoons of lime juice.

4. In a large mixing bowl, toss together the jicama, cabbage, cilantro, and mint. Add the mayonnaise mixture and blend well. Add the corn and edamame and mix well. Season with salt and pepper. Garnish with sprigs of fresh mint to serve.

Serves 6

ingredient note: *Jicama, also known as chop suey yam in Hawai'i, reminds me of water chestnuts with a little bit of sweetness and lots of crunch in its white flesh. Peel the thin brown skin before you use it; eat it raw or cooked (especially good in stir-fry dishes). Find it in supermarkets or Latin markets.*

brie and grape quesadillas
with green pea guacamole

This dish has been on the Hali'imaile General Store menu since day one. I first tasted a version of this at Trumps in Los Angeles and added my twist to a great combination. Who would ever think that green peas would make a great side dish?

CILANTRO-MACNUT PESTO

1/3   cup whole macadamia nuts, toasted

2   cloves whole garlic

1 1/2 cups chopped fresh cilantro

1/3   cup grated Parmigiano-Reggiano cheese

1   teaspoon salt

1/2   teaspoon freshly ground black pepper

1/2   cup olive oil

GREEN PEA GUACAMOLE

1/2   cup chopped red onions

1   jalapeño pepper, seeded and finely chopped

1   tablespoon chopped fresh cilantro

1   teaspoon freshly squeezed lime juice

1   teaspoon ground cumin

Salt

Freshly ground black pepper

3   cups frozen peas, thawed

BRIE AND GRAPE QUESADILLAS

12   (6-inch) flour tortillas

1   cup seedless red flame grapes, halved

6   ounces Brie cheese, thinly sliced

2   tablespoons oil

1. To prepare the pesto, in a food processor, combine the nuts, garlic, and cilantro and pulse until a paste forms. Add the cheese, salt, and pepper and pulse a few times. With the motor running, add the oil through the feed tube and process until the pesto is thick and smooth.

2. For the guacamole, place all the ingredients except the peas in a food processor and pulse until finely chopped. Add the peas and pulse until just blended. Transfer to a serving bowl.

3. Lightly spread 6 flour tortillas with pesto sauce. Top with the grapes and cheese. Top each tortilla with another tortilla and press to hold together. Brush both sides of the quesadilla with oil.

4. In a sauté pan over medium-high heat, place one quesadilla and cook until golden brown. Turn over and cook for 2 minutes to brown the other side. Transfer to a cutting board and cut into 6 wedges. Serve with Green Pea Guacamole on the side.

Serves 6

leftovers? Use leftover pesto with your favorite pasta. Pesto can be stored in an airtight container in the refrigerator for up to 2 weeks or in the freezer for up to 3 months.

grilled chicken panzanella salad

This is one of my favorite salads. (I do have lots of favorite salads!) It's a salad I always order when I see it on a menu, just to see how others prepare it. Some versions allow the bread to be soggy; I like the bread soaked in olive oil. There are lots more ingredients in my version of panzanella, making it a great one-dish meal for lunch or dinner.

6   (6-ounce) boneless chicken breasts

Salt

Freshly ground black pepper

2   cups coarsely chopped tomatoes

1   tablespoon finely minced garlic cloves

$1/2$ cup chiffonade of fresh basil

2   cups extra virgin olive oil

4   cups large seasoned croutons

2   cups cooked white beans (page 164)

1   cup halved $1/4$-inch slices English cucumber

$1/2$ cup halved kalamata olives

1   cup halved thinly sliced red onion

3   tablespoons capers

Zest of 1 lemon

$1/4$ cup fresh lemon juice

2   cups baby arugula

$3/4$ cup shredded Parmigiano-Reggiano cheese

1. Preheat a gas or charcoal grill.

2. Season the chicken breasts with salt and pepper on both sides. Place the chicken breasts skin side down on the hot grill and grill for 4 minutes. Rotate the chicken one half turn to make crisscross grill marks. Cook for another 4 minutes. Turn the chicken breasts over and cook another 6 to 8 minutes until cooked through. Transfer to a platter and keep warm.

3. In a large mixing bowl, add the tomatoes, garlic, basil, and olive oil and toss together. Set aside at room temperature for 30 minutes to allow the flavors to blend.

4. Season the tomato mixture with salt and pepper. Add the croutons and mix well, turning to coat; let soak for 5 minutes. Add the beans, cucumber, olives, onion, capers, and lemon zest and mix well. Add the lemon juice and mix.

5. On a large deep platter, place the arugula. Pour the tomato-bread mixture over the arugula. Slice each chicken breast into three pieces. Place the chicken over the salad. Sprinkle with the Parmigiano-Reggiano.

Serves 6

kālua pork potsticker salad
with grilled pineapple

I created this salad for a dinner we did in Sacramento that celebrated the launch of Hawaiian Air's new route to Honolulu. I wanted a salad that said "Hawai'i!" Grilled pineapple, of course, does this, but it's got to be a Maui Gold pineapple, the sweetest and best-tasting pineapple around. Kālua pork and goat cheese, a perfect combination, reflects the Hawaiian and European food influences in Hawai'i. Wasabi peas pick up the Japanese influence, and there's nothing better than a wasabi vinaigrette to show off the East-West fusion of Hawai'i's food.

KĀLUA PORK

3   pounds boneless pork butt, cut in half

Salt

Freshly ground black pepper

1   tablespoon liquid barbecue smoke

3   cups water

WASABI VINAIGRETTE

3   tablespoons rice vinegar

1   tablespoon soy sauce

1   tablespoon wasabi paste (Japanese horseradish)

1   teaspoon white miso (Japanese soybean paste)

1   teaspoon sesame seeds, toasted

1   teaspoon honey

3/4 cup olive oil

POTSTICKERS

8   ounces soft goat cheese, at room temperature

1   package wonton wrappers

2   eggs, beaten

1   small pineapple, peeled and cored

Peanut oil, for frying

SALAD

8   ounces mixed salad greens

1   carrot, peeled and julienned

1   English cucumber, unpeeled, seeded, and julienned

1   cup wasabi peas

1. Preheat the oven to 325 degrees F.

2. To prepare the kālua pork, place the pork butt in a roasting pan. Season the pork well with salt and pepper. Add the liquid smoke and water to the pan. Cover the pan tightly with aluminum foil and place in the oven. Cook for 2¾ to 3 hours, or until the pork is very tender, almost falling apart. Transfer the pork to another pan and cool. Shred the pork, removing any fat, and measure 3 cups. Any leftovers can be refrigerated or frozen.

3. To make the vinaigrette, place all the ingredients except the oil in a blender and blend at medium-high speed. Slowly add the oil and blend until smooth. Transfer to a covered container and refrigerate until ready to use.

4. Place the pork in a large mixing bowl. With a spatula, blend in the softened goat cheese until well incorporated.

continued on page 172

ingredient note: *To cut vegetables into julienne, first slice them approximately 1/8-inch thick. Stack the slices, then cut them lengthwise into 1/8-inch-thick strips.*

5. To assemble the potstickers, place everything you'll need on a clean and spacious work surface: the filling, wonton wrappers, and eggs. You will also need a pastry brush to apply the egg, and plates on which to put the potstickers after they're made. Dust the plates with flour.

6. Place 6 wonton wrappers on the work surface with point sides toward you. Place 1 heaping teaspoon of the filling in the center of each wrapper. Brush a little of the beaten egg around the outside of each wrapper. Pick up one corner of the wrapper, lift and fold it over the filling, joining it to the opposite corner. Press down along the two sides to form a triangle-shaped potsticker. Place the finished potsticker on a flour-dusted plate. Continue to make potstickers until the filling is used up. Place the potstickers in the refrigerator until ready to fry.

7. To prepare the pineapple, preheat a grill. Slice the pineapple into 1-inch-think slices. Grill the pineapple for about 3 minutes on each side, or until browned. Transfer to a plate and set aside.

8. To fry the potstickers, heat 3 to 4 inches of oil in a large pot over high heat. When the oil reaches a temperature of 375 degrees F, fry the potstickers for 1 minute or less on each side, until light golden brown. The potstickers can be kept warm in the oven until ready to eat but are best when served right after frying.

9. To assemble the salad, in a bowl, toss the salad greens, carrots, and cucumbers with the vinaigrette. Place one slice of grilled pineapple on each salad plate. Top the pineapple with the salad mixture. Sprinkle with the wasabi peas. Place 3 potstickers around the salad.

Serves 6

leftovers? Use leftover kālua pork in sandwiches, quesadillas, wontons, tacos, burritos, omelets, stir-fried with cabbage—the list goes on.

hali'imaile's special lobster salad

One day in the Hali'imaile General Store kitchen, we started throwing together a bunch of ingredients and came up with this salad. It's a dish we put on our menu around the holidays when people want to enjoy something special. I started a love affair with edamame a few years ago—they take the place of frozen green peas that don't do much for me. Plus they're good for you!

SALAD

1¹/₂	pounds cooked lobster meat
1	cup cooked and shelled edamame (green soybeans)
1	cup pear tomatoes, cut in half lengthwise
2	tablespoons diagonally sliced green onions
2	tablespoons coarsely chopped pickled ginger
1	tablespoon chopped fresh cilantro, leaves only
2	teaspoons chopped fresh basil
2	tablespoons chopped fresh mint
6	Lolla Rossa lettuce leaves or other red-leaf lettuce

HERB AÏOLI

¹/₄	cup peeled, roasted, mashed garlic cloves
2	tablespoons minced shallots
2	tablespoons freshly squeezed lime juice
¹/₄	cup chiffonade of fresh basil leaves
¹/₄	cup chopped fresh cilantro leaves
1	cup mayonnaise

SWEET POTATO CHIPS

2	Moloka'i purple sweet potatoes (page 76)

Peanut oil, for frying

Sea salt

1. To prepare the lobster, cut it into ¹/₂-inch cubes and place in a mixing bowl. Add the edamame, tomatoes, green onions, and pickled ginger and mix well. Add the cilantro, basil, and mint and mix well. Refrigerate until ready to serve.

2. To make the aïoli, place all the ingredients in a blender and blend until all the ingredients are incorporated. Refrigerate until ready to serve.

3. To make the sweet potato chips, peel the sweet potatoes. Using a mandoline, cut the potatoes lengthwise into thin slices, about ¹/₁₆-inch thick. Line a plate with paper towels. In a saucepan, heat 2 to 3 inches of oil to 375 degrees F. Place a few sweet potato slices into the oil and fry until very lightly browned, about 2 minutes. Transfer the chips to the plate and drain. Sprinkle lightly with sea salt. Repeat until all of the sweet potato slices are fried.

4. To assemble the salad, line 6 martini glasses with the lettuce leaves so each leaf is sticking out of the glass. Add the aïoli to the lobster mixture and mix well. Divide the lobster salad among the glasses. Garnish with sweet potato chips.

Serves 6

> **ingredient notes:** *Edamame are fresh soybeans, protein rich, delicious to snack on, and a great substitute for frozen green peas. Buy them frozen, with or without their pods, or look for fresh ones in their pods. To prepare them, steam or boil them for about 15 minutes. Drain them, cool, and squeeze out the beans from their pods to eat or use in recipes.*
>
> *Pickled ginger is a staple of sushi bars, thinly sliced young ginger that cleanses the palate and refreshes. It's available in Japanese markets and many supermarkets.*

crispy calamari and spinach salad

Calamari is a food people shy away from until they taste it. If it's cooked properly, people love it for its mild flavor and soft texture. But if you overcook it, calamari can be tough and chewy. Calamari is something I like a lot—the crispy tentacles are my favorite part. By itself, calamari is mild in flavor, so the breading should have lots of flavor.

THAI DRESSING

1	cup rice vinegar
2	tablespoons sugar
2	tablespoons fish sauce
1	tablespoon sambal oelek (Indonesian chile sauce)
1	tablespoon chopped garlic

CITRUS DRESSING

1	cup mayonnaise
1	tablespoon lemon zest
1	tablespoon freshly squeezed lemon juice
1	tablespoon, plus 2 teaspoons Thai sweet chile sauce
1^1/$_2$	tablespoons sugar
2	tablespoons finely chopped fresh basil leaves

Salt

Freshly ground black pepper

CALAMARI

1	pound calamari, cleaned (page 79)
1^1/$_2$	cups all purpose flour
^{3}/$_4$	cup Blackening Spice Mix (page 13)

Peanut oil, for frying

1. To make the Thai dressing, place all the ingredients in a blender and pulse to blend.

2. To make the citrus dressing, place all the ingredients in a blender and pulse to blend. Season with salt and pepper. Pulse to combine.

3. To prepare the calamari, in a colander, rinse the calamari and drain well. Cut off the tentacles, then cut the body into 1/2-inch rings. Repeat with all the pieces of calamari.

4. In a bowl, mix together the flour and the blackening spices.

5. In a saucepan, heat about 3 inches of vegetable oil to 375 degrees F.

6. Place the calamari tentacles into the flour and toss to coat well. Transfer to a strainer and shake off the excess flour. Line a plate with paper towels. Repeat with the calamari rings. In small batches, fry the calamari until golden brown, approximately 2 minutes. Transfer to the plate to drain. Keep warm.

> **ingredient notes:** *Fish sauce, known as* nuoc mam *in Vietnam,* nam pla *in Thailand, and* patis *in the Philippines, is a clear brown liquid that results from fermenting fish with salt for several months. It seems so pungent when you take a whiff, but the fishiness goes away when you cook it. Its saltiness mellows too.*
>
> *Sambal oelek is my favorite chile sauce among the many chile pastes and sauces from around the world. It's a blend of chiles, garlic, and vinegar originally from Indonesia. I like its chunky texture, clean taste, and mellow but distinctive fire. Made in California, this sauce goes well with everything. Mix a little with mayonnaise for a terrific dipping sauce for fried foods.*

SALAD

1   pound baby spinach, cleaned and
    stems removed

¹/₂ cup yellow pear tomatoes, sliced in
    half lengthwise

¹/₂ cup red pear tomatoes, sliced in half
    lengthwise

1   small red onion, sliced into thin rings

7. To assemble the salad, toss the spinach with the Thai dressing in a bowl. Divide the spinach among 6 bowls. Place tomato halves around the spinach. Top with the warm calamari. Drizzle the citrus dressing over the calamari. Place a few onion rings over the calamari and serve.

Serves 6

chopped greek salad

I crave this salad; it's my new favorite. It's the pepperoncini; it's all the flavors mixed together. I serve this in a big bowl at Joe's in Wailea, and next to a wedge of iceberg lettuce with blue cheese dressing (page 179), this salad just hits home. It's simple to make and is a meal in itself.

DRESSING

3/4   cup olive oil

6   tablespoons white wine vinegar

2   teaspoons sugar

1¼   teaspoon Dijon-style mustard

Salt

Freshly ground black pepper

SALAD

1   pound iceberg lettuce, shredded

1   tablespoon finely diced sweet onion

1/2   cup thinly sliced pepperoncini peppers

1   cup capers

1   cup pitted kalamata olives

1   cup crumbled feta cheese

2   tablespoons coarsely chopped fresh dill

1   pound large shrimp, cooked and cut into thirds

24   cherry tomatoes

1   cup halved, unpeeled, thinly sliced English cucumber

1. To prepare the dressing, whisk together all the ingredients.

2. In a large bowl, toss together all the salad ingredients. Add the dressing to the salad, toss well, and serve.

Serves 6

roasted beets and goat cheese salad

Beets and goat cheese are a perfect pairing, arugula adds a zesty note, and everything tastes better with a little bacon!

ROASTED BEETS

¹/₂	pound yellow beets
¹/₂	pound red beets
1	cup golden raisins
1	tablespoon olive oil
1	cup diced onions
¹/₄	pound applewood-smoked bacon

VINAIGRETTE

¹/₈	cup finely diced shallots
1	clove garlic, finely chopped
2	teaspoons Dijon-style mustard
2	tablespoons white balsamic vinegar
2	tablespoons honey
2	teaspoons chopped fresh tarragon
2	teaspoons chopped fresh basil
¹/₄	cup truffle oil

Salt

Freshly ground black pepper

SALAD

8	ounces soft goat cheese
¹/₂	cup breadcrumbs, toasted
3	cups arugula
¹/₂	cup coarsely chopped dry-roasted Marcona almonds (Spanish almonds)

1. To prepare the beets, fill a pot with cold water and add the beets. Over high heat, bring the water to a boil, then reduce the heat to a simmer and cook the beets until they are easily pierced with a knife. Drain the water and set the beets aside to cool. When they are cool, peel the beets, using plastic gloves to keep your hands from staining.

2. Thinly slice the yellow beets and set aside. Cut the red beets into ¹/₂-inch dice. Place the red beets and raisins in a bowl and set aside.

3. In a sauté pan over medium heat, add the olive oil. Add the onions and sauté until caramelized, about 10 minutes. Transfer to the bowl of red beets and raisins.

4. Line a plate with paper towels. In the same sauté pan, fry the bacon until crisp. Transfer the bacon to the plate to drain. Reserve the oil in the pan. When the bacon is cool, chop it into small bits and set aside.

5. To prepare the vinaigrette, in the same sauté pan, over low heat, add the shallots, garlic, mustard, and vinegar and blend together with a whisk. Add the honey. Transfer this mixture to a blender and blend until smooth. Add the tarragon, basil, and truffle oil and blend again. Season with salt and pepper and blend well. Drizzle 2 tablespoons of the vinaigrette over the beets, raisins, and onions and toss together. Place the remaining vinaigrette into a bowl and keep warm.

6. Separate the goat cheese into 8 balls of equal size. With your hands, form the cheese into round flat disks. Roll the disks in the breadcrumbs and set aside.

7. Divide the yellow beets among 8 plates, forming a circular pattern and overlapping the slices. Divide the arugula among the plates, placing

ingredient note: *Arugula or rocket is a soft leafy green with a bitter bite that makes it a wonderful accent in a salad. Baby arugula tends to be milder; older, larger leaves tend to be stronger in flavor. Find arugula at farmers' markets or specialty food stores. Or grow your own in pots!*

it inside the circle made by the beets. On each plate, place a 2-inch ring mold on top of the arugula and pack the red beet mixture into the mold. Remove the ring mold. Place a goat cheese disk on top of the red beets. Sprinkle the bacon and almonds over the plate. Drizzle the warm dressing over the yellow beets. Serve.

Serves 8

wedge *with blue cheese dressing and marinated tomatoes*

As a kid, a wedge of head lettuce was a standard salad and my all-time favorite dressing was blue cheese. The homey, familiar taste of this combination makes it the best-selling salad at Joe's in Wailea. If I'm splurging, I use a French Roquefort cheese for its creaminess and intense flavor; Point Reyes blue cheese from California is a good choice too.

1   **(3-ounce) package cream cheese, at room temperature**

1/2 **cup blue cheese, at room temperature**

1/2 **cup mayonnaise**

1/2 **cup sour cream**

1/4 **teaspoon salt**

1/4 **teaspoon garlic powder**

1/2 **teaspoon Dijon-style mustard**

1/2 **cup whipping cream**

1 1/2 **cups tomatoes (such as cherry, pear, heirloom)**

1   **teaspoon chopped garlic**

1   **tablespoon chiffonade of fresh basil**

1   **tablespoon chopped fresh chervil**

Sea salt

Freshly ground black pepper

2   **heads iceberg lettuce**

16 **strips bacon, fried crisp**

1. In a food processor fitted with a metal blade, add the cream cheese, blue cheese, and mayonnaise and pulse 2 or 3 times to blend together. Add the sour cream, and pulse 2 or 3 times to blend. Add the salt, garlic powder, and mustard. Through the feed tube with the machine running, add the cream. Blend the mixture well.

2. In a bowl, toss together the tomatoes, garlic, basil, and chervil. Season with the sea salt and pepper.

3. Quarter the lettuce heads and remove the cores. Place a wedge on a plate. Pour 2 tablespoons of the dressing over the lettuce. Place 2 slices of bacon over each wedge, crisscrossing the slices. Spoon the tomatoes next to the wedge and serve.

Serves 8

ingredient note: *Chervil is a delicate fresh herb, a member of the parsley family, with curly, dark-green leaves and a hint of anise flavor. Look for chervil where specialty lettuces and herbs are sold.*

Desserts

IT WASN'T LIKE WE HAD DESSERT every night when I was growing up. There was the occasional chocolate cake or brownies from a boxed mix, and fresh peach or strawberry shortcakes made with Pillsbury biscuits sprinkled with cinnamon, sugar, and butter. I remember banana pudding with vanilla wafers and ice cream—we did eat a lot of ice cream in our house and the old crank ice cream maker would often come out. Dessert just wasn't a big deal, and I actually like eating food better than I like eating desserts.

But you have to have desserts in a restaurant. In the early days of Hali'imaile General Store, I didn't have anyone to make desserts. I wasn't going to buy desserts somewhere and serve them, and there weren't even places I could buy them from. So I became the self-taught dessert maker and chalked up more baking disasters than food disasters.

I did get good at a few things like peanut and macadamia nut brittle, cheesecake, and mousse, especially cherimoya mousse. Fortunately I found some brilliant people, including my daughter Teresa "Cheech" Shurilla and my current pastry chef Michelle Kaina, who saved me from being a pastry chef for my restaurants.

Desserts at my restaurants are the desserts I would serve at home. They are not composed, they are not colored with ten different paints, and they are not architectural. They are home-style desserts, just like my food. They are "old-fashioned" American desserts like cobblers, cakes, and pies, tweaked a little to reflect my island home and today's tastes. My desserts are not low in calories or fat—in fact, they're just the opposite, so they taste incredibly good.

Desserts

joe's banana cream pie

I've flown this pie around the country. There was an uprising when I took this dessert off the menu at Joe's in Wailea. This pie just hits home with people: chocolate, caramel, cream, and bananas conjure up warmth, family, and childhood. It has all the flavors we want to eat in a pie.

PIE CRUST

| 20 | Oreo cookies |
| 1/2 | cup butter, melted |

PASTRY CREAM

4	cups whole milk
1	cup sugar
1	vanilla bean, split lengthwise
9	egg yolks
6	tablespoons cornstarch

GANACHE

1 1/2 cups cream

1 1/2 cups semisweet chocolate chips

| 6 | bananas |

Whipped cream, for garnish

Cocoa powder, for garnish

1. Preheat the oven to 325 degrees F.

2. To make the crust, place the cookies into a sealable plastic bag and, using a rolling pin, crush the cookies into fine crumbs. Pour the butter over the crumbs and mix together. Press the mixture into two 10-inch pie pans. Bake for 15 minutes. Remove from the oven and cool.

3. To prepare the pastry cream, heat the milk and 1/2 cup of the sugar in a saucepan over medium-high heat. Scrape the seeds from the vanilla bean and add the seeds and the bean to the milk. In a bowl as large as the saucepan, whisk together the egg yolks, the remaining 1/2 cup sugar, and the cornstarch. When the milk starts to bubble around the edges, add the milk to the egg mixture slowly, whisking constantly. When all the milk has been combined with the egg mixture, pour the mixture through a fine-mesh strainer and back into a clean saucepan. Continue to cook the mixture over medium heat until the pastry cream thickens. Remove the pot from the heat. Pour the pastry cream into a shallow pan and cover with plastic wrap. Plastic should be placed directly on the pastry cream; this will prevent a skin from forming. Cool in refrigerator.

4. To make the ganache, in a saucepan, bring the cream to a boil. Put the chocolate chips in a bowl. Pour the boiling cream over the chocolate and whisk together until smooth.

5. To assemble the pie, pour about 1/2 cup of the ganache into the pie crust and spread. Slice 3 bananas on the diagonal and place the slices on top of the ganache in a circular pattern. Pour another 1/2 cup of the ganache over the bananas, spreading evenly.

6. Pour the pastry cream into a pastry bag fitted with a plain tip. Pipe the pastry cream over the ganache and bananas, filling the crust to the rim. Smooth the surface. Repeat with the second pie crust. Refrigerate the pies to set until firm, about 4 hours. Serve with a dollop of whipping cream and a dusting of cocoa powder.

Makes 2 (10-inch) pies

roasted apple tart *with cornmeal crust*

I always like to have a dessert on my menus that isn't too sweet and features the fruit of the season. This is a rustic, homey kind of dessert for fall; apples and corn go well together. And it's a twist on the all-time favorite apple pie.

APPLE FILLING

8	Fuji apples, peeled, cored, and cut into 8 wedges
1/2	cup firmly packed light brown sugar
1/4	cup butter, melted
1	teaspoon cinnamon

CORNMEAL CRUST

1 1/3	cups flour
1	cup sugar
1	cup cornmeal
1	teaspoon salt
1	cup butter, cut into pieces
3	tablespoons water

STREUSEL

3/4	cup flour
1/3	cup sugar
1/3	cup firmly packed light brown sugar
1/4	teaspoon salt
1/2	teaspoon ground cinnamon
3	tablespoons butter

1. Preheat the oven to 350 degrees F.

2. Line 3 (12 by 18-inch) baking sheets with parchment paper.

3. In a medium mixing bowl, toss the apples with the sugar, butter, and cinnamon. Place the apples on one of the parchment-lined baking sheets in a single layer and bake until tender, about 10 to 13 minutes, stirring apples after five minutes of baking. Remove from the oven and set aside to cool.

4. To prepare the crust, in a large mixing bowl, add the flour, sugar, cornmeal, salt, and butter. Using a pastry blender, cut the butter into the dry ingredients until the mixture resembles peas. Add the water and mix by hand to form a ball. On a floured surface, roll the dough to a thickness of 1/4-inch. Cut out 8 (6-inch) circles. Place four dough circles on each of the two remaining parchment-lined baking sheets; the circles can overlap.

5. To make the streusel, in a medium bowl, toss together the flour, sugar, brown sugar, salt, and cinnamon. Add the butter and cut into the dry ingredients with a pastry blender until the butter is the size of peas. The mixture should remain loose and flaky.

6. To assemble the tarts, place 8 apple wedges in the center of a crust, leaving a 1/2-inch border. Fold the edge of the crust over the apples. Sprinkle the streusel over the top. Refrigerate the tarts for 30 minutes.

7. Preheat the oven to 325 degrees F.

8. Bake the tarts for 15 minutes. Rotate the pans and bake for another 10 minutes or until the tarts are golden brown. Serve warm.

Makes 8 individual tarts

coffee toffee pie

Once we figured out how to make the crust and not have it stick in the pan (see the note below for Perfect Crumb Crust), this pie has been one of the signature desserts at Hali'imaile General Store. It's like eating a candy bar. Thank you, Blum's, for the inspiration.

PIE CRUST

1   package pie crust mix

1   ounce unsweetened chocolate

¹/₄ cup firmly packed light brown sugar

³/₄ cup finely chopped walnuts

1   teaspoon vanilla extract

1   tablespoon water

FILLING

1   ounce unsweetened chocolate

¹/₂ cup butter

³/₄ cup firmly packed light brown sugar

2   teaspoons powdered instant coffee

¹/₄ cup pasteurized eggs

TOPPING

2   cups heavy cream

2   tablespoons powdered instant coffee
     or espresso

¹/₂ cup confectioners' sugar

Coarsely grated or shaved chocolate,
     for garnish

1. Place an oven rack in the center of the oven. Preheat the oven to 375 degrees F.

2. To prepare the crust, measure the contents of the pie crust package; measure half into a large mixing bowl. Reserve the other half for another use.

3. Using a spice grinder, pulverize the chocolate until very fine, or chop it coarsely then grind it in a food processor or blender. Add in the ground chocolate to the pie crust mix. Add the sugar and nuts and toss together. Mix the vanilla and water and drizzle evenly over the pie crust mixture; do not pour it all in one place. Stir with a fork and toss briefly. The mixture will be lumpy and crumbly, but do not try to make it smooth; it will hold together when you press it into place.

4. Press the crust mixture into a 9-inch ovenproof glass pie plate, or follow the instructions below for perfect crumb crusts. Bake the crust for 15 minutes; remove from oven and cool.

5. To make the filling, melt the chocolate in a small bowl over hot water. Set aside to cool.

6. In a bowl, using an electric mixer, cream the butter. Add the brown sugar and beat at moderately high speed for 2 to 3 minutes. Mix in the cooled melted chocolate and the coffee. Add the eggs, one at a time, beating for 5 minutes after each addition, scraping the bowl occasionally with a rubber spatula.

7. Pour the filling into the cooled baked crust. Refrigerate for at least 5 hours or overnight.

8. To prepare the topping, chill a large bowl and electric mixer beaters. Place the cream, coffee, and sugar in the chilled bowl. Using the mixer with the chilled beaters, whip the cream until the cream holds a definite shape, but do not overbeat; the cream should be firm enough to hold its shape when the pie is served, but it should remain slightly creamy rather than stiff. Spread the whipped cream smoothly over the filling, or apply it in fancy swirls using a pastry bag fitted with a large star-shaped tip. Sprinkle grated or shaved chocolate over the top. Refrigerate until ready to serve.

Makes 1 (9-inch) pie

PERFECT CRUMB CRUST

Although a crumb mixture may be pressed into place directly in the pie plate, I prefer to line the plate with foil first and then remove the foil before filling the crust. This guarantees easy serving—the crust can't stick to the plate.

For a 9-inch pie plate, use a 12-inch square of aluminum foil. Place the plate upside down on a work surface. Place the foil over the plate and, with your hands, press down on the sides of the foil, pressing it firmly against the plate all around. Remove the foil. Turn the plate right side up. Place the shaped foil into the plate. Using a potholder or a folded towel, press the foil firmly into place in the plate, making sure that the foil touches all parts of the pan. Fold the edges of the foil down over the rim of the plate.

Turn the crumb-crust mixture into the plate. Using your fingertips, distribute the mixture evenly and loosely over the sides first and then the bottom. Then press the crust firmly and evenly on the sides, pushing it up from the bottom to form a rim slightly raised over the edge of the plate. Be careful that the top of the crust is not too thin. To shape a firm edge, use the fingertips of your right hand against the inside and press down against it with the thumb of your left hand. (Lefthanders can use opposite hands throughout this procedure.) After firmly pressing the sides and the top edge, press the remaining crumbs evenly and firmly over the bottom. There should be no loose crumbs.

Bake the crust in the center of a preheated 375-degree-F oven, according to the recipe instructions. Cool to room temperature.

Transfer the pie plate to the freezer and freeze for at least 1 hour or longer, until frozen solid. Remove from the freezer. Raise the edges of the foil. Carefully lift the foil with the crust from the plate. Gently peel away the foil as follows: Support the bottom of the crust with your left hand and peel the foil, a bit at a time, with your right hand. As you do so, rotate the crust gently on your left hand.

Supporting the bottom of the crust with a small metal spatula or a knife, ease it back into the plate very gently so as not to crack it. It will not crack or break if it has been frozen sufficiently.

kona mud pie

When I first moved to Hawai'i, I had a mud pie at the Chart House in Honolulu and loved it. This is my version of it: a chocolaty crust, brownies, and coffee ice cream, and then I top it with hot fudge sauce. The best thing is that you can make this dessert, keep it in the freezer, and have dessert for a few days. That is, of course, if it doesn't get eaten the first night!

BROWNIES

1/4	cup butter
2	ounces semisweet chocolate chips
2	eggs
1	cup sugar
1/2	teaspoon vanilla extract
1/2	cup flour
1/4	teaspoon salt
1/2	cup diced macadamia nuts

PIE CRUST

2	cups Oreo cookie crumbs, about 12 cookies
1/4	cup butter, melted

1/2 gallon coffee ice cream

Hot fudge or caramel sauce, for garnish

Whipped cream, for garnish

1. Preheat the oven to 325 degrees F.

2. Grease and flour a 9 by 9-inch cake pan.

3. To prepare the brownies, in a microwavable bowl, melt the butter. Stir in the chocolate to melt the morsels and blend together.

4. In a large mixing bowl, using an electric mixer, beat the eggs, sugar, and vanilla for 1 minute, or until well blended. Add the melted chocolate and beat until the chocolate is incorporated. Mix in the flour and salt until well blended. With a rubber spatula, fold in the macadamia nuts. Pour the mixture into the pan and bake for 25 to 30 minutes.

5. Remove the brownies from the oven; keep the oven on. Cool the brownies, then cut them into 1/2-inch squares and set aside.

6. To prepare the crust, in a medium bowl, mix the Oreo crumbs and butter. Press the mixture into the bottom of a 10-inch springform pan. Bake for 7 minutes. Remove from the oven. Cool, then place the crust in the freezer until frozen.

7. To make the filling, cut the ice cream into small chunks. (This will help prevent straining the mixer.) In a large mixing bowl, using an electric mixer with a paddle attachment, add half of the coffee ice cream chunks and turn the mixer on. Mix for 1 minute, then add the rest of the chunks slowly. Continue to mix until the ice cream is smooth.

8. Using a rubber spatula, fold the brownie chunks into the ice cream, being careful not to smash up the brownies. Pour the ice cream mixture into the Oreo crust, smoothing the top. Return the pan to the freezer and freeze overnight.

9. To serve, release the sides of the springform pan and transfer the pie to a serving plate. Cut the pie into wedges and serve with hot fudge or caramel sauce, and whipped cream.

Makes 1 (10-inch) pie

sour cream-rhubarb pie

A favorite dessert of my husband, Joe, is rhubarb pie. So when the rhubarb pops up in my backyard (yes, it's cool enough in Upcountry Maui to grow rhubarb), we have rhubarb pie on the menu.

PIE CRUST

2¹/₂ cups flour

¹/₂ teaspoon salt

¹/₂ teaspoon baking powder

1 cup butter, cold, cut into ¹/₂-inch cubes

4 to 6 tablespoons cold water

TOPPING

²/₃ cup quick-cooking oatmeal

6 tablespoons firmly packed light brown sugar

6 tablespoons bread flour

Pinch of cardamom

2 teaspoons lemon zest

4 tablespoons butter

FILLING

1¹/₂ cups sugar

¹/₃ cup flour

1 cup sour cream

4 cups peeled and diced rhubarb

Vanilla bean ice cream

1. Preheat the oven to 325 degrees F.

1. To make the crust, place the flour, salt, and baking powder in the workbowl of a food processor outfitted with the metal blade. Pulse 3 times to mix. Add the butter and pulse several times until the mixture resembles coarse cornmeal. Scatter 4 tablespoons of water over the mixture and pulse 5 times. The dough should begin to hold together. If it is still crumbly, add 1 tablespoon of water and pulse again, repeating if necessary until the dough holds together. Remove the dough from the workbowl, form a disk, and wrap in plastic wrap. Refrigerate for 1 hour.

2. When the dough is firm, remove it from the refrigerator, unwrap it, and roll it into an 11-inch circle. Spray a 9-inch pie pan with vegetable oil. Transfer the dough into the pie pan. Flute the edges of the crust and shape to desired look. Line the crust with parchment paper, completely covering the bottom and sides of the crust with a single piece. Fill the crust with raw rice or beans. Bake the crust for 15 minutes. Remove the pan from the oven and gently grab the four corners of the parchment paper, lift it and remove it from the crust. Return the crust to the oven another 5 to 7 minutes, or until light brown. Remove the crust from the oven and set aside.

3. To make the topping, in a large mixing bowl, add the oatmeal, brown sugar, bread flour, cardamom, and lemon zest. Add the butter and using a pastry blender, cut the butter into the dry ingredients until the butter is the size of peas. The topping mixture should be loose and flaky. Set aside.

4. To make the filling, in a medium mixing bowl, whisk together the sugar, flour, and sour cream until smooth. Add the rhubarb and mix. Pour the mixture into the pie shell.

5. Sprinkle the topping over the rhubarb. Bake for 50 to 55 minutes. Remove the pie from the oven and cool for about 30 minutes to set. Cut and serve with a scoop of vanilla bean ice cream.

Makes 1 (9-inch) pie

peach-blueberry cobbler
with shortcake biscuits

There's nothing better than eating a fresh peach, juice dripping down your chin. So I'm always on the search for great peaches and when I find a batch, peach cobbler is on the menu. You can use frozen peaches and blueberries for this recipe, but be sure to use IQF (individually quick frozen) fruit.

SHORTCAKE BISCUITS

3¹/₂ cups flour

³/₄ cup sugar, plus additional sugar for sprinkling

2 tablespoons baking powder

4 hard-cooked egg yolks, mashed

6 tablespoons butter

1¹/₂ cups heavy cream

COBBLER FILLING

10 fresh ripe peaches, peeled, pitted, and cut into 8 wedges

2 cups sugar

1 cinnamon stick

³/₄ cup cornstarch

1 cup water

2 cups fresh blueberries

Whipped cream or vanilla ice cream, for garnish

1. Preheat the oven to 300 degrees F.

2. Line 2 (12 by 18-inch) baking sheets with parchment paper.

3. To make the biscuits, in a large mixing bowl, toss together the flour, ³/₄ cup sugar, baking powder, and cooked egg yolks. Add the butter and using a pastry blender, cut the butter into the flour mixture until the butter is the size of peas. Add the cream and knead by hand until the dough comes together and forms a ball.

4. On a floured surface, roll the dough to a thickness of 1 inch. Using a round 3-inch cookie cutter, cut out the biscuits. Place 4 to 5 biscuits on each baking sheet and sprinkle each with sugar.

5. Bake for 20 minutes; rotate the pans in the oven and bake for 10 minutes more. The biscuits will be golden brown and the centers should be cakelike. Remove the biscuits from the oven and set aside.

6. To make the cobbler filling, in a large heavy-bottomed pot over medium heat, cook the peaches, sugar, and cinnamon stick for about 10 minutes or until the peaches are tender. Drain the peaches, reserving the juice. Remove and discard the cinnamon stick. Set the peaches aside. Return the peach juice to the pot and bring to a boil over high heat.

7. In a small bowl, whisk together the cornstarch and water to create a slurry. Quickly whisk the slurry into the peach juice. Continue to whisk until the mixture becomes thick like a pie filling. Cook for 5 minutes. Remove the pan from the heat and fold in the peaches and the blueberries.

8. To serve, split a biscuit in half and place a scoop of the warm filling across the bottom half of biscuit. Place the top half of the biscuit over the cobbler and top with a dollop of whipped cream or serve with vanilla ice cream.

Serves 8

pineapple upside-down cake

Located in the middle of pineapple fields on Maui, we simply must have a pineapple dessert at Hali'imaile General Store. For this nostalgic dessert, we use the Maui Gold, a low-acid sweet pineapple grown by Maui Land and Pineapple Company. This is just a simple, homey dessert but one that everyone loves. You can make this in a cake pan or individual ramekins—your choice.

1   large fresh pineapple

CARAMEL

³/₄   cup butter

2   cups firmly packed light brown sugar

CAKE

1¹/₂ cups sugar

6   tablespoons butter

8   egg yolks

¹/₂ cups cake flour

1   tablespoon, plus ¹/₂ teaspoon baking powder

¹/₂ teaspoon salt

1   cup whole milk

2   teaspoons vanilla extract

1. Preheat the oven to 300 degrees F. Have ready a 9 by 13-inch rectangular baking pan or 9 (8-ounce) ramekins.

2. To prepare the pineapple, remove the skin and trim off the top and bottom. Slice the pineapple into 9 thick rings. Remove the core from each slice. If you are using ramekins, trim the pineapple rings to fit the ramekin. Set aside.

3. To make the caramel, in a saucepan over medium heat, melt the butter. Add the brown sugar and stir until the mixture becomes smooth. Remove from the heat and set aside.

4. To make the cake, in a large mixing bowl with a hand mixer, cream the butter and the sugar for 3 minutes. Add the egg yolks and mix for 1 minute on medium speed.

5. Sift the cake flour, baking powder, and salt together. Add the flour mixture to the butter-sugar-egg mixture and mix on low speed to incorporate. Scrape down the sides of the bowl with a spatula and mix for another 30 seconds. Slowly add the milk, scraping down the sides of the bowl again. Add the vanilla, and mix for another 30 seconds.

6. Spread the caramel evenly over the bottom of the pan or ramekins, leaving no empty spaces. Place the pineapple rings on top of the caramel. Pour the cake batter over the pineapple, leaving a 1-inch space from the top of the pan or ¹/₄ inch from the top of the ramekin.

7. Place the ramekins on a baking sheet; place the pan or the ramekins in the oven and bake for 35 minutes. Rotate the pan or ramekins and bake for another 10 minutes. Bake until the center of the cake is cooked or when a cake tester comes out clean. Remove from the oven, cool for 5 minutes. Carefully invert the pan or ramekins and release the cake onto a serving plate.

Serves 9

chocolate decadence torte

It's dense but it's not too rich. You be the judge.

³/₄   **cup butter**

8   **cups (3 ¹/₂ pounds), semisweet or bittersweet chocolate chips or chopped pieces**

12   **eggs**

¹/₃   **cup sugar**

²/₃   **cup cake flour, sifted**

¹/₂   **cup heavy cream**

Raspberry purée or a fresh berry compote, for garnish.

> ingredient note: *In our restaurants, we use a bittersweet chocolate that has 58% cacao content. It's a chocolate we buy in big chunks, unlike the chocolate you find in supermarkets. For this recipe and the Kona Mud Pie (page 188), I recommend a semisweet or bittersweet chocolate that has a cacao content close to 58%. Baker's makes a semisweet chocolate with 54% cacao content; Ghirardelli makes a bittersweet chocolate with 60% cacao content.*

1. Preheat the oven to 300 degrees F.

2. Grease a 10-inch round cake pan and line the bottom with parchment paper.

3. In a large microwavable bowl, melt the butter on high for 1 minute. Add 7 cups of the chocolate to the melted butter and whisk until the chocolate is completely melted and smooth. You may have to return the bowl to the microwave for 1 minute at a time until the chocolate is completely melted, stirring at each minute interval. Leave the chocolate in the microwave to keep it warm.

4. In a large bowl, using an electric mixer with a whip attachment, beat the eggs on high speed for 5 minutes. Add the sugar and continue beating on high speed for 20 minutes, during which time the eggs will double in volume and become thick.

5. When the eggs are ready, using a rubber spatula, fold in the warm chocolate mixture. Slowly fold in the flour, being careful to not create lumps. When the flour is well blended, pour it into the cake pan. Place the cake pan into a larger pan. Fill the larger pan with hot water halfway up the sides of the cake pan. Bake in the oven for 55 minutes.

6. Remove the pans from the oven, and then remove the cake from the water bath and set aside, cool to room temperature. Chill in the refrigerator for 30 minutes. Invert the pan onto a flat surface and tap the edge of the pan until the torte pops out of the pan. Place the torte on a serving platter and refrigerate for two hours.

7. To make the ganache, place the cream and the remaining 1 cup of chocolate in a microwavable bowl and heat for 1 minute in a microwave. Stir with a fork until the chocolate is melted and smooth.

8. Remove the torte from the refrigerator and pour the warm ganache over the top of the torte. With a spatula, spread the ganache evenly over the whole torte. Chill for 10 minutes to set the ganache.

9. Cut into wedges to serve, garnishing with a raspberry purée or a fresh berry compote.

Makes 1 (10-inch) torte

hali'imaile blueberry cheesecake

Cheesecakes are a guilty pleasure. But this one takes away some of the guilt because blueberries are good for you! Blueberries have the highest antioxidant activity among fruit and can help fight off chronic diseases associated with aging. Now I'm all for that!

CRUST

2	cups graham cracker crumbs
1/2	cup sugar
2	tablespoons butter, melted

CHEESECAKE

4	(8-ounce) packages cream cheese, at room temperature
1²/₃	cups sugar
1²/₃	cups sour cream
3	eggs, beaten
1	cup puréed fresh blueberries
Zest of 1/2 lemon	
1	cup whole fresh blueberries

1. Preheat the oven to 300 degrees F.

2. Spray a 10-inch springform pan with cooking-oil spray. Cover the outside bottom and sides of the springform with aluminum foil. The cheesecake will be baked in a water bath, so it is important that the foil be one piece completely covering the bottom and ending at the top of the pan.

3. To make the crust, in a bowl, mix together the cracker crumbs, sugar, and butter. Mix well to moisten the crumbs. Press the mixture into the bottom of the pan. Bake for 10 minutes. Remove the pan from the oven and set aside to cool. Decrease the oven temperature to 250 degrees F.

4. To prepare the cheesecake, using an electric mixer with a paddle on medium speed, beat the cream cheese and sugar until the mixture is smooth and there are no lumps. Scrape down the bowl and paddle, and mix again for one minute. Add the sour cream and mix on low speed until the sour cream is incorporated. Scrape down the bowl and paddle again.

5. Add the eggs, puréed blueberries, and lemon zest. Mix on low speed for one minute. Remove the paddle, scraping it and the sides of the bowl. Using a rubber spatula, fold in the whole blueberries.

6. Pour the mixture over the crust. Place the pan in a larger pan. Fill the larger pan with water halfway up the sides of the smaller pan. Bake for 1 hour and 30 minutes. The cheesecake is done when the center is set or when a cake tester inserted into the center comes out clean. Remove the cheesecake from the oven and the water bath. Cool to room temperature, then chill for 2 hours before serving.

7. Release the sides of the pan to unmold the cheesecake and slide it onto a serving plate.

Makes 1 (10-inch) cheesecake

vanilla crêpes *with caramelized bananas and tropical fruit salsa*

Dessert crêpes are one of my favorite things; they're simple, elegant, and easy to do. Make a batch of crêpes ahead of time and freeze them; pull them out and fill them with whatever fruits are available, or sauté them in butter with a flavored liqueur. Crêpes are light, not too sweet, and I think they're coming back into fashion.

FRUIT SALSA

1   mango, peeled, seeded, and cut into ¼-inch dice

1   strawberry papaya, peeled, seeded, and cut into ¼-inch dice

Half of a large pineapple, peeled, cored, and cut into ¼-inch dice

CARAMELIZED BANANAS

¼   cup butter

1   cup firmly packed light brown sugar

1   tablespoon cinnamon

10   bananas, peeled and cut into ½-inch slices

CRÊPES

1½   cups milk

3   egg yolks

2   tablespoons vanilla extract

1½   cups flour

2   tablespoons sugar

½   teaspoon salt

5   tablespoons butter, melted

1. To make the salsa, in a medium bowl, mix the mango, papaya, and pineapple together. Cover and refrigerate until ready to serve.

2. To caramelize the bananas, in a skillet over medium heat, melt the butter. Add the brown sugar and cinnamon. Cook until the butter and sugar blend together and becomes creamy; do not boil, which will cause the butter to separate. Add the bananas and cook for 1 minute, stirring constantly. Remove from the heat and set aside.

3. To make the crêpes, in a large bowl, whisk together the milk, egg yolks, and vanilla. Stir in the flour, sugar, salt, and melted butter and mix until well blended.

4. Heat a 12-inch sauté pan over medium heat until hot. Lightly coat the pan with oil. Pour ¼ cup of the batter into the pan, immediately tilting and swirling the pan to cover the entire bottom surface of the pan. When the crêpe starts to bubble and the edges start to brown, loosen the edges with a spatula and flip the crêpe over. Cook the crêpe for an additional minute, or until lightly browned. Transfer the crêpe to a plate. Repeat with the remaining batter.

5. Divide the caramelized bananas evenly among the crêpes, fold or roll into desired shape, and place 2 on a serving plate. Top with fruit and serve.

Serves 6

liliko'i brûlée *in an almond brittle shell*

Making tuiles (or shells) is not easy, and this almond brittle tuile will not be different. The tricky part is getting the just-baked shells onto the glass bottoms at just the right moment. But make a batch, plan to lose it (you can still enjoy the crumbs), and then make another batch, which will be perfect. Unlike other crème brûlées, this one is made on the stovetop like a pudding, which it is—a very creamy, silky pudding.

ALMOND BRITTLE SHELL

6   tablespoons butter, melted

²/₃ cup light Karo syrup

1¹/₂ cup sliced almonds

¹/₄ cup, plus 1 tablespoon bread flour

³/₄ cup sugar

BRÛLÉE

2   cups heavy cream

³/₄ cup sugar

1¹/₂ cups egg yolks (about 12 to 15 yolks)

¹/₂ cup liliko'i (passion fruit) purée

Additional sugar, for garnish

Fresh berries such as strawberries, blueberries, raspberries, or blackberries, for garnish

1. Preheat the oven to 300 degrees F.

2. Line 2 (12 by 18-inch) baking sheets with parchment paper. Lightly oil or spray the bottoms of 6 (8-ounce) glass cups. Set the glasses aside, oiled bottoms up.

3. To make the shells, in a mixing bowl, using an electric mixer with a paddle attachment, mix the butter, Karo syrup, almonds, flour, and sugar for three minutes. The mixture will be thick and bind together like dough. Divide the mixture into 8 balls. Place 4 balls on each baking sheet, spacing them evenly as they will double in size as they bake. Lightly flatten each ball to ¹/₄-inch thick disks. Bake one pan at a time for 15 to 20 minutes, or until golden brown.

4. Remove the pan from the oven and immediately cut the parchment around each almond brittle so that the disks are separated from each other. Let the disks sit for 1 minute, then flip them onto the glass bottoms to create a free-form shell. Let the shells cool on the glasses, then store them in an airtight container until ready to use.

5. To make the brûlée, prepare an ice bath, filling a large bowl (double the size of the saucepan you will be using) halfway with ice. Add water to cover the ice. Set aside.

6. In a large, heavy-bottom saucepan over medium-high heat, bring the cream and sugar to a boil.

7. While the cream comes to a boil, beat the egg yolks in a medium bowl. You will need to temper the yolks and cream to prevent the yolks from scrambling and becoming lumpy. To do this, using a 4-ounce (¹/₂-cup) ladle, add hot cream to the yolks while whisking the mixture vigorously. Repeat this process three times. (Some cream will remain in the pot.) Then pour the cream-yolk mixture through a fine-mesh strainer into

continued on page 200

ingredient note: *Liliko'i is the Hawaiian name for passion fruit, an egg-shaped tropical fruit with yellow or purple skin. The soft, seed-studded flesh has a sweet-tart flavor that's vibrant and aromatic. I like to use liliko'i in place of lemon juice in recipes for curds, tarts, and pies. Look for fruit that has a dimpled, almost shriveled skin, indicating that it's ripe. Find liliko'i at farmers' markets in Hawai'i and in Latin markets in the mainland United States.*

the pot of boiling cream, whisking vigorously again. Continue to cook the mixture, whisking the entire time.

8. When the mixture is thick like a pudding, immediately remove the pot from the heat and place it into the ice bath to stop the cooking. Add the liliko'i purée and stir until the purée is mixed in. Cool the mixture in the ice bath, stirring occasionally. Cover and refrigerate for two hours to set the brûlée.

9. To assemble the dessert, place the shell in the center of a plate and scoop the brûlée into the shell. Sprinkle the brûlée with sugar and, using a small kitchen or crème brûlée torch, toast the sugar until brown and caramelized. Be sure the flame touches just the sugar and not the shell. Scatter fresh fruit around the shell and serve.

Serves 8

key lime martini

I love Key lime pie, but it's a dessert you have to make and serve the same day to be really good. So we have each part of the pie ready to put together when it's ordered. If you can find Key lime juice, use it. Otherwise we get great results with fresh Hawaiian limes.

KEY LIME FILLING

3   (14-ounce) cans sweetened condensed milk

²/₃ cup egg yolks (about 6 to 7)

1¹/₄ cups fresh squeezed lime juice

CRUST

³/₄ cup graham cracker crumbs

2   tablespoons butter, melted

¹/₂ cup sugar

Fresh berries or seasonal fruit, for garnish

1. Preheat the oven to 300 degrees F.

2. To make the curd, in a large bowl, whisk together the condensed milk, egg yolks, and lime juice. Pour the mixture into an (8 by 8-inch) square cake pan. Place the pan in a larger pan. Fill the outer pan with hot water halfway up the sides of the smaller pan.

3. Bake for 25 minutes or until the curd wiggles and holds together like Jell-O. Remove the pan from the oven and the water bath, cool to room temperature, and refrigerate for 2 hours to set the curd.

4. In a small bowl, mix the cracker crumbs, butter, and sugar and set aside until the dessert is ready to be assembled.

5. To assemble the dessert, divide the crumbs evenly among six martini glasses. Scoop the curd onto the crumbs. Sprinkle berries or fresh fruit over the top and serve.

Serves 6

pick-up sweets:
chocolate-dipped macaroons, coconut-raspberry bars, and basic cookies

When Celebrations caters a party, we always serve pick-up sweets at the end of a meal, a selection of one- or two-bite cookies or other sweets in a variety of flavors. These are few of our pick-up sweets—obviously they can each stand on their own as dessert. The recipe for Basic Cookies with variations is especially handy when you want to make an assortment of flavored cookies.

CHOCOLATE-DIPPED MACAROONS

¹/₂   cup butter, at room temperature

1¹/₄ cups sugar

2   eggs

2¹/₂ cups sweetened, shredded coconut (Angel Flake preferred)

2³/₄ cups desiccated coconut (macaroon coconut)

³/₄   cup cake flour

1   bag chocolate candy melts (dipping chocolate)

1. Preheat the oven to 300 degrees F.

2. Line 4 (12 by 18-inch) baking sheets with parchment paper.

3. In a mixing bowl, using an electric mixer with a paddle attachment, cream the butter and sugar on high speed for 5 minutes. Add the eggs and mix on low speed to incorporate. Scrape the sides of the bowl and paddle. Add the coconut and the flour, and mix on low speed until they are well blended. Do not overmix.

4. Using a #70 ice-cream scoop, form the dough into balls, and place them on baking sheets. Bake for 15 to 20 minutes, or until golden brown. Remove the macaroons from the oven and cool on the baking sheet.

5. Melt the chocolate candy according to the directions on the bag. Dip each macaroon half way into the chocolate and place each one back on the baking sheet. When all the macaroons have been dipped, place them in the refrigerator for a few minutes to set the chocolate. Transfer the macaroons to an airtight container for storage.

Makes 66 (5¹/₂ dozen) cookies

COCONUT-RASPBERRY BARS

³/₄   cup butter, at room temperature

2¹/₃ cups sugar

2   eggs

4¹/₄ cups cake flour

1   teaspoon salt

10   cups coconut

1¹/₂ cups seedless raspberry jam

1. Preheat the oven to 300 degrees F.

2. Line a 12 by 18-inch baking sheet with parchment paper.

3. In a large mixing bowl, cut the butter into the sugar using a pastry blender or a fork until the butter is the size of peas. Blend in the eggs by hand. Add the flour, salt, and coconut and using the pastry blender, mix the ingredients together. Do not overmix; overmixing will cause large lumps to form. The mixture should stay loose and flaky.

4. Transfer half of the mixture to the baking sheet and press into the bottom. Bake for 15 minutes, or until the top is golden brown. Remove from the oven and immediately spread the jam over the crust. Top with the rest of the crust but do not press down. Bake for 18 minutes, or until the top is golden brown. Remove from the oven and cool. Cut into 3-inch squares. Store in an airtight container.

Makes 24 (2 dozen) bars

continued on page 204

BASIC COOKIES

1   cup butter, at room temperature

1   cup firmly packed light brown sugar

1   cup sugar

2   eggs

1   teaspoon vanilla extract

3   cups flour

1   teaspoon baking soda

1/2   teaspoon salt

1. Preheat the oven to 375 degrees F.

2. In a medium bowl with a mixer on low speed, cream together the butter, brown sugar, and sugar until well blended. Add the eggs and vanilla and mix well.

3. Sift together the flour, baking soda, and salt. Add to the butter mixture in batches until well mixed. Add additional flavor ingredients listed below, if desired.

4. Using a 1-ounce scoop (2 tablespoons), portion the cookie dough onto a baking sheet. Place in the oven and bake for 12 to 15 minutes, or until golden brown. Remove from the oven and cool on a wire rack. Store in an airtight container.

VARIATIONS: *For Oatmeal, Cranberry, Raisin Cookies:* Add 2 cups quick-cooking oatmeal, 1 cup dried cranberries, and 1 cup golden raisins.

For Chocolate Chip Pecan Cookies: Add 2 cups semisweet chocolate chips and 2 cups chopped pecans.

For Macadamia Nut Double-Chocolate Cookies: Add 2 cups toasted diced macadamia nuts, 1 cup dark chocolate chips, and 1 cup white chocolate chips.

H·FLOW

BANANA
BREAD

THESE ORIGINAL BOUQUETS ARE
PICKED AND MADE DAILY! ONLY
$7⁰⁰ EA. BOUQUET.
YOU ARE PERMITTED TO CARRY
THESE ON THE PLANE TO HAWAII.
TO PROLONG THEIR LIFE (UP TO 3
WEEKS) KEEP OUT OF DIRECT SUN
CHANGE H₂O EVERY THREE DAY
KEEP BOUQUET IN A BAG FOR
STEMS. THEY WILL DO FINE
WITHOUT H₂O FOR YOU GET TO
THE OTHER SIDE.
ENJOY! MAHALO.
PLEASE TAKE THIS CARD TO
ORDER MORE WHEN YOU GET
HOME... WE'LL SHIP ANYWHERE!

Index

About the Author

BEVERLY GANNON is one of Hawai'i's top chefs, well respected as the chef and owner of Hali'imaile General Store, Joe's in Wailea, and Celebrations Catering, all on the island of Maui.

Bev was born and raised in Dallas, Texas. After high school, she got the travel bug and eventually became road manager for various entertainers. While on the road, she met her future husband, Joe Gannon, but it wasn't until 1980 that they moved to Maui and married. By then, Bev had taken some serious cooking classes in Europe.

Life on the beach on Maui was punctuated by informal catered parties for friends and celebrities visiting the island. Then in 1984, Bev got the bug to start a business that would use her skills and creative talent in the kitchen. Celebrations Catering started in her home and garage, and word of mouth helped expand her clientele and repertoire. When Hali'imaile General Store became available four years later, Bev took the old plantation store that was two miles from her home and transformed it into what was going to be an upscale take-out deli.

But on opening day in October 1988, Bev realized that people wanted a sit-down restaurant, and that is what it became. Hali'imaile General Store is a casual, family friendly, but upscale, restaurant with a menu that focuses on fresh Maui-grown foods prepared in Bev's inimitable style that blends the flavors and techniques of Texas, the American South, Hawai'i, and Asia. Bev's motto has always been "It has to taste really good."

In 1995, Bev opened Joe's in Wailea, Maui, where Joe Gannon's favorite comfort foods are the focus. Celebrations Catering continues to provide fine foods for business and corporate meetings, weddings, holiday and family celebrations on Maui and throughout the state of Hawai'i.

Bev and her restaurants have received numerous accolades and awards throughout the years. She was a founding member of the Hawai'i Regional Cuisine chefs, a group of a dozen chefs who put Hawai'i on the culinary map through their commitment to using locally grown foods in preparations that reflected Hawai'i's heritage. In 2004, Bev was nominated for the James Beard Foundation's Best Chef, Hawai'i and Northwest Region, Award.

Bev is the corporate chef for Hawaiian Airlines, where her signature style is reflected in meals throughout the aircraft. She also oversees the menu and kitchen of Lana'i City Grill on the island of Lana'i. Topping off a spectacular career, Bev was named the Hawai'i Small Business Administration's Small Business Person of the Year in 2008.